Manor

Moira Buffini's plays include *Blavatsky's Tower* (Machine Room), *Gabriel* (Soho Theatre), *Silence* (Birmingham Rep), *Loveplay* (Royal Shakespeare Company), *Dinner* (National Theatre and West End), *Dying for It*, adapted from *The Suicide* by Nikolai Erdman (Almeida), *A Vampire Story* (NT Connections), *Marianne Dreams* (Almeida), *Welcome to Thebes* (National Theatre), *Handbagged* (Tricycle Theatre and West End), *wonder.land* (National Theatre) and *NW Trilogy* (Kiln Theatre). Screenplays include *Jane Eyre*, *Tamara Drewe*, *Byzantium* and *The Dig*.

MOIRA BUFFINI

Manor

faber

First published in 2021
by Faber and Faber Limited
74–77 Great Russell Street
London WC1B 3DA

Typeset by Brighton Gray
Printed and bound in the UK by CPI Group (Ltd), Croydon CR0 4YY

A CIP record for this book
is available from the British Library

978-0-571-36331-5

2 4 6 8 10 9 7 5 3 1

For Bridie, Maya, Joe and Jack,
the next generation

Acknowledgements

I'd like to thank all at the National Theatre Studio, where I wrote the first draft of the play in three intense weeks, especially Emily McLaughlin for her steadfast support. Thank you to my friends and family, for reading the play around my kitchen table as it began take shape. It made such a difference to have you all on board. Thanks to Isabel Lloyd for some great early notes. Thanks also to the actors who workshopped the play with me; your input was invaluable. Thank you Rufus Norris for steering the play into production, and for keeping faith in it through the long months of lockdown. Thanks to St John Donald for bringing order to the storm, and to Dinah Wood and Steve King, without whom I'd be ephemeral. I am very grateful to our company of actors, who have given so much integrity and fine detail to the characters. Most of all, my thanks to Fiona Buffini. A pleasure, as always, watching you work.

Manor was first performed in the Lyttelton auditorium of the National Theatre, London, on 16 November 2021. The cast was as follows:

Ripley Michele Austin
Anton Peter Bray
Diana Nancy Carroll
Isis Liadán Dunlea
Ted Shaun Evans
Ruth Amy Forrest
Fiske David Hargreaves
Perry Edward Judge
Pete Owen McDonnell
Dora Shaniqua Okwok

Understudies
Ripley Sophie Cartman
Anton Lewis Griffin
Diana Helen Barford
Isis Sophie Bradley
Ted/Perry Mat Betteridge
Ruth Gillian Dean
Fiske/Pete Chris Barritt
Dora Effie Ansah

All other parts played by members of the company

Director Fiona Buffini
Set and Costume Designer Lez Brotherston
Lighting Designer Jon Clark

Composer and Sound Designer Jon Nicholls
Video Designer Nina Dunn
Fight Director Kate Waters
Dialect Coach Majella Hurley
Company Voice Work Jeannette Nelson and Victoria Woodward
Associate Set Designer Louie Whitemore
Associate Costume Designer Diane Williams
Associate Sound Designer Beth Duke
Staff Director Sepy Baghaei
Casting Directors Sam Jones CDG & Isabella Odoffin CDG

Characters

Diana Stuckley
Lady of the Manor

Pete Stuckley
her husband

Isis Stuckley
their daughter, twenty

Reverend Dominic Fiske

Judith Ripley
a nurse

Dora Ripley
her daughter, eighteen

Ted Farrier
an extremist

Anton St Hilaire
his aide

Ruth Getz
Ted's fiancée, an academic

Perry Gould
currently unemployed

Setting

A manor house near the British coast. Present day.

MANOR

Act One

SCENE ONE

Late afternoon. Light sinking. Rain hammering.
A partial rendering of a manor house in a sodden British landscape.
Great Hall: staircase, stone fireplace, hint of diamond leaded windows. Shabby detritus of generations; rifles, guitars on stands. A couple of manky stuffed animal heads, one with party string still hanging from it. At the top of the staircase, two photographs: Diana in her modelling days, Pete with his band, Capital.
Another area hints at a kitchen: old-fashioned stove, big table, couple of exploding armchairs. No door between the two areas.

Isis Stuckley is at the kitchen table, working. Laptop, pile of bills. The strain, in her sensitive eyes, of being the only adult in the house.
Her father, Pete Stuckley, is in the Great Hall, cleaning a pair of rifles. Semi-dancing to the music on his headphones. His background is working class. He sings an occasional line and starts using one of the rifles as a guitar.
Diana Stuckley comes down the stairs. Still traces of the 'It girl' she once was. She is carrying a bucket. She takes it to the front door, tips it out and puts it under a dripping leak.

Diana Pete

Diana moves into his line of vision.

Pete

Pete removes a headphone.

3

I've used all the buckets and big pans
    There's leaks in almost every room.
    I need you to help me

Pete With what?

Diana The flood's right up to the edge of Schott's field
    We need to get out there and protect the wedding barn

Pete I'm busy

Diana With what?

Pete Art

Diana Oh come on

Pete (*turning back to his gun*) My object's the gun of Empire.
Lee-Enfield; standard First World War issue. Your great-grandad probably shot deserters through the throat with these

Diana The barn might flood. Will you please help me?

Pete What for?

Diana We haven't paid the insurance

Pete We can't stop this. It's biblical

Diana Useless relic. And I don't mean the gun

Diana goes into the kitchen. Pete sets up a camera on a tripod.

He won't help

Isis He's trying to create and it's hard

Diana Everything's hard when you're bone idle

Isis He's depressed

Diana He's lazy

Isis He was in here making tea and he said that any response to these weather events is futile. He said it was like a man trying to shoot a cloud to get it to stop raining. And I said 'That's good, Dad, that's a profound image.' So he's going to go outside and film himself shooting at the sky, until the camera itself is destroyed by rain

Diana I'm quite stunned by how pointless that is

Isis It's supposed to be pointless, that's the point

Diana We need to get out there and sandbag the wedding barn

Isis With what?

Diana Sandbags

Isis We haven't got sandbags

Diana There should be people out there, delivering sandbags in trucks
We should've foreseen; we should have sandbags
Why haven't we got sandbags?

Isis Are you blaming me for not ordering sandbags?

Diana manages to stop herself from saying yes.

The water's never come up that far, not in any flood. I know the river's burst its banks but I think the sea-wall would have to breach

Diana It's pouring into those fields

Isis The barn's higher

Diana Is it?

Isis Yes

Diana Am I over-worrying?

Isis I hope so

Diana This weather's making me feel nuts. I feel completely mad. Sorry

Isis Shall I make some tea?

Diana Thank you

Isis puts the kettle on.

Everything's stirred up
I put a bucket in the yellow room
And I heard the tapping
So quietly, like a little hello

Isis Did you provoke it?

Diana No
Yes

Isis I wish you'd leave it alone

Diana It's in there, brewing
Making mottled patches on the wallpaper
They're growing, like fungal thrush
All that cloud pressing down, this weird gloom –
No wonder it's woken

Diana taps on a surface.

Isis Can you not do that please?

Diana You shouldn't be scared of it

Isis I'm not

Pete has finished setting up his camera.

Diana Days and days of rain
The damp is in my teeth
Saturated ground, this overwhelming sky

Isis The teapot's full of magic mushrooms

Diana Oh. Oh God

Isis He's in there playing with guns

They go to the door. Pete is preparing one of the rifles.

Diana We're not going to panic. We won't panic

Isis What shall we do?

Diana I think we should let him flare up and go under

Isis What if it gets like last time?

Diana draws Isis away from the door.

Diana There's nothing he can do without bullets and after the Jehovah's Witness incident I've got them hidden where he'll never look

Isis Where?

Diana In a tampon box

Pete puts a tampon box on the table.

Isis What if he turns? He might turn

Diana Last time he only turned because of that God-awful home-made Calvados. I tipped the whole lot away. There's not a single bottle left

Pete swigs from a bottle of home-made Calvados. He loads a rifle.

Isis What if he hurts himself?
What if shooting at the clouds is just a ploy?
What if he actually wants to die?

Diana is genuinely troubled by this thought.

Diana Pete would never do that.
Besides, have you seen what he's wearing. He'd never choose to meet Death in that. There was a time when I'd have been in there with him, dancing like a banshee. I'd have ripped off his shirt and licked his chest

Isis Can you not?

Diana When he's peaked we'll put him to bed.
How are the accounts?

Isis We need to deal with him, Mum

Diana No, come on, the Chandhras' wedding must have made a difference. And the Birnbaums'. If we had one of those every weekend we'd be flying

Isis We're not flying. It's wrong that we're scared to go in there

Diana That wedding barn is going to save us. We can start looking to the future

Isis We've only got four bookings for the spring. We need to have a wedding every fortnight or we can't repay the loan. The Chandhras only gave us three stars

Diana That's his fault; it's *his fault*
   He's sabotaging all our efforts
   He walks in and thinks the young people have heard of him
   He drinks their champagne and tries to sing his hit

Isis It's not just him. You're snobby and unwelcoming and people can tell

Pete fires his gun at a china fireside dog. He misses.

Pete Bastard Porcelain Shit

Diana No

Diana and Isis recover.

Isis I'm going to phone someone. We need help

Diana Who would come?

Pete I'm going to finish you, you little sods

Isis Get him upstairs
   I'll make him some food

Diana Bastard

Isis Don't provoke him

Pete You should be fucking landfill

Pete fires the rifle. Misses. Diana goes into the Great Hall.

Diana What are you doing?

Pete The scope's off, but it fires like a dream. Bolt-action beauty

He fires at another ornament. It explodes.

Yes, Yes

Diana That's my Pongo

Isis is trying to make a call. She has no signal. She multitasks by making an emergency sandwich.

Pete Ugly objects with no use or meaning.
I was going to go outside and fire up into the sky
Give it to the jet stream, to the unfolding chaos –
But that chaos started here, in rooms like this

Diana What are you talking about?

Pete Centuries of Empire, military capitalism

Diana Oh don't

Pete The industrial subjugation of the world
War, slavery, the dance of an elite –

Diana Leave my stuff alone, you bullshit prick

Pete It all connects. We're at the heart of a system that's destroyed the very air

Diana Give me back my gun

Pete Our gun
Until we divorce
Then I'm going to rip your manor house apart

Diana No you fucking won't

Diana grabs the gun. They struggle for it.

You've fed on me

Pete You fed on *me*
You took my flame and tried to warm your freezing heart

Isis enters.

Diana You took my youth –

Pete Your heart, made from the stone of your manor –

Isis Mum

Diana You preening one-hit wonder

Isis Dad

Pete Everything in here should be destroyed

Isis I made a sandwich

The adults notice her. Pete lets go of the gun.

Pete Isis

Isis Everything's okay, Dad. There's some food here

Pete What are you doing, looking like that?

Isis Like what?

Pete It can't be you

Isis What's wrong with me?

Pete You break my heart

Isis Why?

Pete Look at you
We should never have had you

Diana Oh God

Pete The world's heyday is over
You've been born too late

Isis Sit down and eat

Pete I've lived so carelessly
      I've been a heedless prince, an oblivious flâneur
      And here we are at the End of Days

Isis Eat this

Pete I haven't helped you, haven't told you, haven't given
you the tools
      The world's about to be consumed by the system that we
live in

Isis Yes

Pete You know that to be true
      We're past the point of no return

Isis I know

Pete We've unleashed the desert and the storm
      Our greed will kill us all

Diana Tripe

Pete Tripe, is it?
      Is it tripe, Diana?

Isis Please eat some of this

   Pete sits with Isis and the sandwich.

Pete Your grandad was a socialist

Isis I know

Pete Union man through and through
      He saw all humans equal
      Except toffs. He thought they were scum

   Diana angrily rolls her eyes.

It was clear in those days
      It used to seem so clear
      There was us
      And scum

Isis Explain when you've eaten

Pete My grandad fought in the Spanish Civil War,
    He used a gun like that to fight fascists
    He fought and he lost
    But his fight had meaning.
    I sold myself
    I've been intoxicated and seduced
    I'm a traitor to my kind
    And what does that make you?
    You've not stood a chance
    No wonder you've come out wrong

Isis Don't

Pete You're a beautiful miscreant, Isis

Isis puts the sandwich down.

Isis You're such a mess. I hate you

Isis goes into the kitchen. Pete looks to Diana.

Pete It's pointless going on

Diana Come upstairs

Pete We should end this horror

Diana There's a lovely bed. You can lie down

Pete I've got business with that sturdy rifle

Diana Let's do something else

Pete All of our finest achievements have been in the service
of death.
    Death's our muse, our inspiration. We worship death
    Death – we worship you

Lightning. The lights go out.

Diana Damn

Pete I did that

Diana It's a power cut

Pete No it isn't
  I worshipped death and the lights went out

  Diana lights a candle. A long rumble of thunder.

I made it dark
  Death is bequeathing me power
  I'm its votary, at the crux of the storm
  And my primal force put the lights out

Diana Come and look at this, Pete

Pete Why?

Diana I want you to see something

  Diana draws him up the staircase, holding a candle.

Pete You slink around my ankles like a cat
  You play with me, all soft and slinky.
  You're getting your claws ready, aren't you

Diana Look

  *She brings him to the framed posters of their youth. Pete
  stares, dismayed. A low tapping sound can be heard
  intermittently.*

We were quite the couple, weren't we?

Pete Why are you showing me this? Those people are dead

Diana No, no, we're still here
  Come and rest
  We were always on the same side

Pete Which side is that?

Diana We were both rebels

Pete You don't know the meaning of the word

Diana Come and lie down

Pete Lie down and die?

Diana Just get some fucking sleep

Pete You're going to put me in that yellow room

Diana I'm trying really hard

Pete You're a fucking spider and this is your lair

Diana Don't turn on me, Pete

Pete You're a slow killer
You stupefy your prey

Diana I'm just trying, really gently –

Pete To pounce

He grabs Diana tightly by the wrist.

Diana Let me go

Pete You and this house; you're not benign. You're eating me alive

Diana You're hurting me – Let go

Pete You've been sucking my sap for twenty years

Diana Isis is scared of you and so am I

Pete You've got me like a stuffed head on your fucking wall

Diana You're full of shit

Pete You'd cheer if I was dead

Diana burns Pete's throat with the candle, to make him let go. He cries out – knocking the candle out of her hand. They glare at each other. Diana pushes Pete as hard as she can.
    Pete falls all the way down and lies, inert.
    The low, intermittent tapping stops. Diana comes down, consumed with fear.

14

Halfway down the stairs she stops. An upstairs door slams. A presence passes her. She clutches her arm, as if she has felt it. She is afraid.

Diana Pete. Get up

She touches him. The rain intensifies.

Come on, Pete. Let's stop this

Panic grips her.

(*Shouts.*) Isis – Isis –

Isis is stuffing her face with bread. She spits it into the bin and enters. She sees.

Isis What happened?

Diana He fell

Isis goes to Pete. She examines him with the light from her mobile phone.

Isis Dad

Diana He was hurting me

Isis What were you doing?

Diana Just trying to contain him. He was gripping me –

Isis Did you push him?

Diana No – no – he hurt me

Isis He's burnt

Diana I put the candle against his neck to make him let go
He stepped back
And there was nothing there

Diana puts her hand out for Isis's phone.

We need help

Isis There's no signal

Isis listens to his chest.

He's dead

Diana He's not dead

Isis He's not fucking breathing, Mum

Diana takes his pulse.

Diana He's dead

Isis goes for the landline.

I didn't push him
You have to believe me
Say you believe me

Isis There's nothing
There's no one

The rain hammers down.

SCENE TWO

Later. Relentless rain. Candles, rusty oil lamps. The Great Hall is lit; the kitchen in darkness. Isis is opening the door to Dominic Fiske, the vicar, in Lycra, Gore-tex and dog collar.

Fiske Hello, Stuckleys. Very glad you're in

Diana Dominic, come by the fire

Fiske River's come right through the kitchen. I'm awash

Judith Ripley and her daughter Dora enter, clutching wet bags.

Diana Oh, that's awful

Ripley (*to Isis*) Hi

Isis Hi

16

Fiske Brought some fellow refugees
  These are the Ripleys

Ripley Hello

Fiske Judith took the stables at Pear Tree Cottage

Ripley For a long weekend

Fiske Same thing there, I'm afraid

Ripley Within half an hour it was up to our shins. This is my daughter, Isadora

Fiske Diana and Isis

  A handshake Diana barely meets.

Ripley Everyone just calls me Ripley. So sorry to impose on you

Isis Shall I take your wet things?

Fiske We met trying to get our cars out. Had quite an adventure. The bridge is washed away

Isis Oh my God

Ripley The river's massive; it was so frightening

Fiske So we turned around and tried the coast road; treacherous

Diana Is the sea-wall holding?

Fiske The tide's freakishly high. The waves are crashing over the top, like huge things. (*He is giving an impression of their size.*) We came back

Ripley Down on the lane it was above our knees

Diana No

Ripley We didn't know where else to come

Dora We could have stayed in Balham

Ripley Can we not do this?

Dora I'm wet to my actual knickers and I nearly fucking died

Ripley I had hold of you

Dora All the other cottages were empty because they had Wi-Fi. They could see what was coming

Ripley I banned her phone and she's angry

Dora I'm not angry, this is PTSD – and you didn't ban my phone; I'm not ten. You booked a place in the middle of nowhere with no Wi-Fi

Ripley I thought it would be nice to be off our phones, just for a day

Diana Maybe I'll get some towels

Diana takes a candelabra and goes into the kitchen, where Pete's body is laid out, under a sheet on the table. She takes some towels from a pile of clean laundry. She pauses, looking at the corpse.

Fiske The Lord's decided to stir us all up

Isis It's not the Lord, is it. It's the Earth, trying to throw us off her back

Fiske Well you see, when you characterise the Earth like that, don't you think it's just the same as saying God?

Isis If God exists, he's sending this weather cos he hates us

Fiske Isis

Isis You need to come

Isis pulls Fiske into the kitchen.

Dora This is so shit

Dora cries. Ripley pulls her into her arms.

18

Ripley It's all right. I was scared too

In the kitchen, Fiske is looking at the shrouded corpse.

Fiske Pete

Ripley I'm so sorry

Diana He was high as a kite. He fell downstairs. We couldn't call anyone

Dora I lost my coursework

Ripley But we're fine

Dora My bag with all my work

Ripley We're somewhere safe. Everything'll be okay

Fiske I'm so sorry

Ripley It's just the shock

Dora That fucking water

Ripley Try to calm the swearing, in front of them

Dora 'Everyone calls me Ripley'?

Ripley I'm just trying to be friendly

Dora Why?

Diana returns with the towels. Fiske is lifting the sheet.

Ripley Diana, this is so kind of you. Could we help with anything?

Diana No, I don't think so

Ripley We checked the weather before we left London. All it said was rain
   And I thought 'Fine, I'll make it nice and cosy, we can study by the fire'
   We've both got exams you see and we badly needed to get away

I'm studying at work and Dora's got her A levels
looming, so

Dora She's not interested, Mum

Isis (*to Fiske*) I said I hated him
But I don't
I don't

Fiske takes Isis in his arms. Diana is on the landing.

Diana My husband was in this band when he was young.
Capital
They were just before The Libertines
They were almost The Libertines

Ripley Wow, what's his name?

Diana Pete Stuckley
'Love Will Heal Our Scars'
That's his hit

Ripley I was probably listening to other stuff

Diana It got to number three
Where did you say you were from?

Ripley Balham

Diana I once had a flat in Notting Hill
I don't think I ever went south of the river

Diana exits upstairs.

Dora Is she cussing South London?

Ripley She's from the country; they all hate London

Dora More than that. She doesn't want us in her creepy-ass
house

Ripley I think she's in some kind of state

Dora No; she doesn't like us. This place is haunted. Let's go
and sleep in the car

Ripley Are you kidding? Freak weather kills people

Dora There's worse ways to die. She's going to come down and make us recite something backwards and then this, like, hell-mouth is going to open –

Ripley We're her guests. And there are rules about that. So button it, Miss Thing

Dora Don't ever make me come to the countryside again

Diana appears on the landing carrying quilts and pillows. In the kitchen, Fiske holds Isis.

Fiske It's been a great sadness to me,
Watching your father over the years
I think it's hard to be an artist in this world
He had success too young, too briefly
And was still searching for his purpose.
We have to forgive him, Isis

Ripley takes some bedding from Diana.

Ripley Let me help you

Diana It's all a bit damp, I'm afraid. I'd offer you a bedroom but they're freezing. We don't heat them

Ripley We'll be fine here, thank you so much

She follows Diana as Dora lays out the quilts and pillows on two armchairs.

It's a lovely, atmospheric house

Diana Yes

Ripley Is it Tudor?

Diana It dates from the Restoration

Ripley Is that like big, long wigs?

Diana Yes

Ripley Could I trouble you for a hot-water bottle, for Dora?

Diana Of course

Ripley I did try to tell her to bring a warmer coat but, you know
   She's actually more fragile than she looks
   My marriage ended not so long ago and

Diana How funny, so did mine

Ripley This weekend was like an opportunity for us to

Dora Are you telling her our shit?

Diana My husband's dead, as a matter of fact

Ripley Oh

Diana He fell downstairs and killed himself. He's on the kitchen table

   Dora sits, dazed at how awful her weekend is. Fiske appears.

Ripley I'm so sorry
   There must be something we can do

Fiske Ripley, Dora, my friend and neighbour Pete has died
   Diana, shall I say some words?

Diana Yes

Fiske Would you all gather round?

   Fiske takes Diana into the kitchen.

Dora Just let me sleep in the car – please

Ripley Someone has died, so get a grip
   It matters how you behave
   We're the Ripleys of Balham
   You can do this

   Dora rises to the occasion. They follow the others into the kitchen.

Fiske Pete, go forth from this world
In the love of God the Father who created you
In the mercy of Jesus Christ who redeemed you
In the power of the Holy Spirit who strengthens you

A distant tapping can be heard.

May the heavenly host sustain you
And the company of heaven enfold you.
May you dwell this day in peace
Amen

All Amen

Diana We tried to call an ambulance

Ripley He fell down your stairs?

Diana Yes

Isis We couldn't leave him lying there

Fiske Ripley could have a look at him. She's a doctor

Diana It's a bit late. Isn't it

Ripley I'm actually a Nurse Practitioner. I'm training to be a doctor so

Fiske I thought you were a doctor

Ripley No; many more exams before I get the title. I work at King's in Camberwell

Fiske She should look at him, Di

Diana What on earth for?

Fiske There's a protocol. Ripley can pronounce him dead and what-have-you

Ripley Would you like me to? Then when the emergency services arrive, you'll know that someone has done all they can?

Isis Thank you

Fiske I know this is super-tough

Diana No. Fine. Whatever you like

Diana draws Isis away as Ripley lifts the sheet. Ripley regards Pete. The tapping again.

Isis It's tapping

Diana No it isn't

Isis I wish it would shut up

Ripley Is that a singe on his neck?

Diana I don't know

Ripley His skin's blistered

Diana Yes

The rain is exceptionally heavy now.

Ripley How did that happen?

Diana We were lighting candles and he'd had a lot to drink

Ripley Were you there when he fell?

Diana Of course I was there

Ripley I'm sure in the morning, help will come, but if you could bear to tell me what happened?

Diana He was climbing the stairs and we stopped at the top and he said he was channelling the storm or death or something and he said he'd caused the power cut with his will. He was very drunk. And he stepped backwards and missed his footing

Ripley And the burn?

Diana Yes, he had a candle

Isis I thought you had the candle

Diana He took it. He snatched it quite childishly and he stepped back

Ripley Why?

Diana I don't know why, he was off his box on magic mushrooms. The sink's still full of them, you can go and look

Ripley So he burnt himself?

Dora Mum it's not your business

There's a hammering on the front door.

Diana Would you excuse me?

Diana rapidly covers the corpse again. She walks through the Great Hall at speed. She opens the door. Ted fills the doorframe (his confidence making his stature seem greater than it is), supported by Anton (a small-town boy who has found a balm for his wounds in extreme politics). Both are drenched to the skin but well dressed in expensive coats and dark shirts.

Ted Thank fuck
We saw your light

He and Anton shut the door. Ted limps; his ankle is injured.

Our car hit the water in your lane
There's a fucking river down there
Your lane turns into a river

Anton We were almost / swept away

Ted All you had to do was follow Chris

Anton I did my best

Ted Your shit fucking driving nearly killed us
You had Chris in front and Darren behind

Anton I couldn't see them
  I couldn't see the road
  And you were yelling

  *Fiske has entered, unnerved by the swearing and
  aggression. Ripley, Isis and Dora follow.*

Ted This is your fault

Anton You can't blame me for the weather
  I checked my app and this isn't the weather it said
  The symbol just said rain

Ted What's the symbol for nuclear winter, Anton?

Anton It's the ionising radiation symbol on a snowflake

Ted Smart-arse little fucker, aren't you?

Fiske I know it's treacherous out there but please could you
temper your language

Ted A vicar

Fiske This is Lady Stuckley's home

Ted Unreal

  Ripley recognises Ted.

Anton We've got to go back out. Our friend, Ruth, she's
still in the car

Diana Why didn't you bring her up with you?

Anton We had to be sure we'd find shelter

Ted She's blind

Anton It's his fiancée. She got hurt

Fiske Good heavens

Anton We have to go out and get her

Ripley Right. I'm with you

Fiske Wellies on

Isis Mum, come on

Anton There's other people out there. We saw a fat bloke clinging to a hedge

Ripley (*to Dora*) You're not coming

Dora I'm not leaving you

Isis I'll get a rope and torches

Fiske We'll all be knights in shining Gore-tex

They all start preparing, except Diana and Ted.

Anton We were in the golf hotel
The waves were battering
Like at reception they were saying that the tide –
There's some storm way out at sea and it's massively swelling the tide
And this river estuary burst its banks
So water started coming under the doors and everyone was leaving
They said the sea-wall was going to breach
And the conference just cleared right out
Then as we were driving
All this water
That coast road

Ted We've lost two cars

Diana (*to Isis*) The barn will flood. We'll lose the barn

Isis It's insured, Mum

Diana No. I didn't pay

Isis takes this in, angry.

Isis There's people out there

Anton Come on, Ted

Ted You go back out. You play the hero
    My ankle's fucked, thanks to you

Isis, Anton, Ripley, Dora and Fiske leave. Ted remains.

Aren't you going with them?

Diana No

Ted You're able-bodied. There's a fat bloke in need out there

Diana Why would I leave you alone in my house?

Ted I see. Got me down as a thief, have you?

Diana Some kind of criminal, yes

Ted I'm a lawbreaker, that's true
    But I've just been through a near-death experience
    My brothers, my loyal brothers are lost
    I'm standing here soaked
    Clearly in physical pain
    I don't get a towel, a cup of tea
    You don't even invite me to sit
    That's criminal, lady

Diana I don't care about your loyal brothers
    They're probably as vile as you
    I'll never tiptoe through my house again
    Because a man sees fit to throw his weight around.
    You want tea?
    Fuck off
    I don't like you
    So when your lackey brings your poor, deluded girlfriend back
    You can sit this rain out in my garage

Ted I've got to warn you, I'm a stranger in need. There are laws about that and you're breaking them. *Xenia*: Ancient Greek. My deceitful girlfriend told me all about it – and being blind, she relies on it a lot. Hospitality was a religious obligation to the Greeks. They believed that gods walked among them and if they abused a stranger, they'd be at grave risk of abusing a god

Diana So you must know about *hubris*? It's what happens when men compare themselves with gods. My husband met his earlier, when he said he'd caused a power cut with his will. Come, I'll introduce you

Diana leads Ted into the kitchen. She introduces him to Pete.

This is Pete. Pete – I'm sorry I don't know your name?

Ted Is this a joke?

Diana Is there a circumstance in which it would be funny?

Slowly, Ted lifts the sheet. He looks at Pete. Then at Diana.

When we met, he was the love of my life

Ted lowers the sheet.

Ted Look, I apologise. I apologise. Sometimes my manner can be too

Diana Repugnant

Ted Impassioned
Let me make the tea
You sit down
In fact, fuck the tea
Let's start again
I'm very sorry for your loss

Diana I'm feeling nothing

Ted That's normal, they say. When I've lost people I've felt nothing too

Diana I feel like I'm floating an inch off the ground
A weird detachment

Maybe it's a dark euphoria
Something seismic has changed

Ted Could I make you a drink?

Diana I don't keep much in the house. That's his home-made Calvados. It's disgusting

Ted Would you like one?

Diana Yes

Ted What happened to him?

Diana He fell downstairs. He was an alcoholic

Ted pours two drinks.

Ted My mum was an alcoholic
Her culture was defective in that way; Irish
She drank Campari
Hate the smell of it, I hate it still
When I smell Campari I react
You know what I mean? Like a hot sweat, like

Diana Buried trauma

Ted I just think anyone who drinks it should be killed

Diana Where are you from?

Ted England's belly

Diana What a weird thing to say

Ted My town's a collection of estates linked by roundabouts. What about you?

Diana There's rotting portraits of my ancestors upstairs

He hands Diana the drink. She sips it.

Ted I'll take that as *xenia*. In letting me fix your drink, you've just said 'Make yourself at home'. The Romans called it *hospitium*

Diana *Hospitium*

Ted That vicar called you Lady. Is that an actual title?

Diana Yes, it's on my Tesco Clubcard if you want to check

Ted You married the Lord of the Manor?

Diana The title's mine. Pete was from Stockport. My badboy, for a while

Ted What's your name?

Diana Diana Stuckley

Ted You're Lady Diana?
  Well fuck me

  Diana considers Ted.

Diana How's your ankle?

Ted Throbbing

Diana I'm going in by the fire

  Diana goes back into the Great Hall. Ted follows, bringing the Calvados.

Ted May I say what a startling house this is
  Candlelit, feature fireplace
  Like being in a slasher film
  Is it Gothic?

Diana No

Ted Was that an ignorant question?

Diana It's Restoration

Ted What's that then, ruffs?

Diana Lace, feathered hats. It came out of the ashes of the Civil War, literally. The Parliamentarians burnt the old place down

Ted Parliamentarians. They've always been wankers

Diana It's called Burnt Marple. I do a guided tour on the first Thursday of every month

Ted I forget this country had a civil war
There's a gap in my historical knowledge, you see.
It goes World War Two, Napoleon, Crusades, Rome.
Not much use for Restoration
I like the sound of it though
Restoring things to how they should be

Diana The river's burst its banks
The sea-wall's breached
I'm alone, looking at the future
And the storm is here

She puts her fist against her heart.

Ted My heart got pulled out of my chest today
There's gore now, dripping down my front
D'you understand that?
I've been deceived

Ted breathes deeply. The wind rises.

You need to find your wrath

Diana My what?

Ted Your strength
Make it hot steel
And send it out to hit its mark.
That's how you look to the future

Diana You're a very curious person

Ted I'm exceptional
I can say that to you because you're exceptional too
You're off the scale
Not just because of your fancy manor and your Tesco Clubcard;

You're above the norm; outstanding
Is it unnerving to hear that?

Diana It's what I was taught from an early age

Ted I bet it was. But even you
You're not supposed to say the difficult truth: I feel my
own superiority
You shine

Diana Ha
People used to say that when I was young. I was a model,
for a while

Ted I can feel the light coming off you

Diana I find other people dull
Most people are so dull

Ted There are two kinds of people, aren't there?
You know what I'm going to say
You're already agreeing
There are those who never question, those who like to
obey
And those who are audacious, who dare, who can
transform

Diana I felt that way when I was twenty
I could do anything

Ted It took me time to find my power,
To look around and say
I'm better than these lazy, boring, desperate, unwelcome
people

Diana My father used to say 'There's us – and the rest'
And I rebelled, thinking 'No, you're wrong, we are All
One'
I can feel him tonight, laughing at me
Tonight, when it's too late

Ted Too late for what?

Diana I'm going to lose this house.
  I haven't honoured what I am
  That's what my father would say
  And this flood will finish me

Ted I think a tornado wouldn't stand a chance with you

Diana I'm wondering if you're a con man

Ted Con men fail because they never tell the truth. I do
  Everybody lies, everyone's a salesman
  But I'm not
  If I think it I will say it and my thoughts don't flinch
  Underneath those clothes I bet your skin is white as snow

Diana That poor woman you abandoned in your car

Ted No, you don't mean that
  You're already wondering what I'd be like.
  My grandpa would have tugged his forelock to the likes
of you.
  He'd have beaten your grouse.
  I'd like to beat your grouse

Diana Get me another drink

Ted What would you like?

Diana I'd like a fucking big one

Ted My pleasure

  *Ted pours drinks. A strange noise from upstairs; a door
  slamming.*

Is there someone upstairs?

Diana There's been a dwelling here for over a thousand
years. It was once a Norman motte-and-bailey castle.
There's a yellow room that's cold, even on a summer's day.
A door-slamming presence abides in there. She passed me
on the staircase earlier; dug her pointed elbow right into my
side, the dead bitch

Ted Fuck her. Here's to the living

They drink.

Diana You haven't told me your name

Ted Farrier. Ted Farrier

Diana Why does that mean something to me?

Ted Albion

Diana Is that a pub you run?

Ted Google me

Diana How? The barge that brings the internet has come
adrift. The world is being swept away

Ted I knocked on your door and it's a motte-and-bailey
castle

Diana Farrier; you'd have shod our horses

Ted You are pure England. You're the lady in the lake

Diana Soon to be homeless

Ted I could help you

Diana Have you got money, Ted?

Ted Yeah
And something better
Power
I had my DNA done
Forty per cent Celt, fifty per cent Saxon
The final ten per cent – Italian
That's from the Romans. I'm a Roman

Diana All-conquering

Ted Sometimes, the best thing for civilisation, is to give in
to the invasion

They are about to snog. The door opens, bringing in Isis. She clocks their intimacy before they part. Anton and Ripley enter, with Ruth between them. Ruth is bleeding from her leg and back.

Ruth Ted
Ted

Anton She was in the water

Ruth Where is he?

Anton She'd got out of the car. She was in the lane, screaming

Ruth Why did you leave me? I could have died. The water was filling the car

Anton You're safe now

Ruth Ted

Ted I'm right here

Diana She can perch by the fire

Ripley She's in shock – she needs blankets

Isis I'll get her a hot-water bottle

Isis goes into the kitchen. Ripley brings Ruth to a chaise. Anton brings a quilt for her.

Ruth Ted, how could you abandon me?

Anton You're okay

Ted You were safe in the car. We had to leave you

Ruth It wasn't safe, you stupid lumpen ass
I don't know what you think you saw, you jealous, paranoid bastard
You knew I was injured and you left me in that car to drown

Ted You're embarrassing yourself

Anton She's bleeding pretty badly, Ted

Ripley Let's get these things off. We'll soon have you warm

Anton and Ripley help Ruth onto a chaise.

Diana I'm not being funny but that's an antique chaise

Ripley Do you have any dry clothes?

Diana Yes of course

Dora and Fiske enter, helping an obese man, Perry. Diana shuts the door.

Fiske Diana, this is Perry

Perry Fucking hell

Fiske He was in a spot of bother

Perry Fucking hell
Fucking hell

Fiske So sorry, seem to be

Fiske half faints.

Perry Oh shit
Fucking hell

Diana Dominic

Diana assists Dora. They lead Fiske to a chair. Isis returns with a hot-water bottle.

Here, come and sit

Isis hurriedly gives the hot-water bottle to Perry and goes.

Perry You all right?

Fiske Yes

Perry I couldn't see you. I didn't realise you were so fucking old

Ripley (*to Dora indicating Ruth*) Go to her.
Dominic, are you in any pain?

Fiske No no

Perry Fucking hell

Ripley (*loosening Fiske's collar*) Do you feel any constriction in your chest?

Fiske No

Perry Fucking hell

Ripley Any tightness or tingling?

Fiske No

Ripley What about in your arms, any pins and needles?

Fiske No. Just light-headed

Perry Fucking hell

Ripley Any pain going into your jaw or neck?

Fiske No

Ripley Good. Stay very still and take deep, slow steady breaths

Perry Fucking hell

Ripley (*returning to Ruth*) Dora, everyone needs hot tea. Diana – towels, quilts, blankets, whatever you've got, dry socks, any more clothes. Take your wet things off, people. Wrap up if you can. (*To Anton.*) You – sort the fire

> *Anton does so. Dora follows Isis into the kitchen. They look at the corpse. Dora makes a gesture of comfort. Isis accepts it. Then they get on with making tea.*

Ted You like to be in charge, don't you?

Ripley I need my bag

She points. Ted gets Ripley's bag.

Twenty-one years in A&E, so this wound of yours, Ruth, is my daily bread

Perry (*to Diana*) I've always wondered what this house was like. Didn't think I'd nearly have to peg it to get in

Ripley I need to warm my hands

Diana Here

Diana takes a hot-water bottle from Perry and gives it to Ripley. She goes upstairs.

Ruth Ted
Ted

Anton He's right by you

Ruth puts out her hand for Ted.

Ruth I need you

Ted No you don't

Ted moves away.

Ripley Ruth, it'll hurt less if I cut you out

Ripley brings some scissors out of her bag. Ted watches, still as a heron as she cuts Ruth's top.

Ted You must have had a busy time of it recently

Ripley (*shouts*) Dora, boiling water to sterilise. Is there a first-aid kit?

Isis looks for a first-aid kit. Ripley cuts.

Ted I said you must have been busy

Ripley I've been triaging people in ambulances when they can't get in the door

Ted That's very laudable

Ripley It's not laudable. It's a travesty and an outrage and an offence

Fiske Hear, hear

Perry Fucking hell

Perry is staring at Ruth's injury.

Ripley How did you get injured?

Ted She fell into the water by the car

Ripley Ruth can tell me

Ruth There was something down there. Something went into my back. Stuck into my back. Here

She gestures towards her shoulder.

Ripley In the water?

Ruth Yes, when I fell

Perry She's bleeding, I nearly died, you're having a stroke; fucking hell

Fiske I'm not having a stroke; I'm absolutely fine

Diana is coming downstairs with a pile of clothes, including a dressing gown and socks.

Perry I was in my caravan
    I saw the river rising but I wouldn't leave my tech
    And I thought, you know, a normal flood; it's usually okay
    But the whole thing
    It lifted up on the water
    It was moving
    Water coming in
    It was tipping
    I got out

I was clinging to the hedge
I left my medication, everything
I didn't even lock it

Fiske That's very bad

Diana You picked a jolly bad weekend to go caravanning

Perry What?

Diana Awful timing to visit your caravan

Fiske I don't think Perry was visiting

Perry I fucking live there
I know your husband
I've had chats with him

Diana None of this will fit you

Diana goes upstairs to get more sheets and blankets.

Ruth Tell me your name

Ripley Judith Ripley

Ruth Don't leave me on my own with him

Ripley I won't

Ripley is examining Ruth's wound with the light from her phone. Dora comes in with a first-aid kit.

(*To Dora.*) Brilliant. Thank you. I need to clean the wound and stitch it. Could you help?

Dora nods. Isis holds out some mouldy bread.

Isis On my survival course they said that mouldy bread was full of penicillin

Ripley Yes
I need a clean sheet on here.
I need painkillers – everything you've got

Dora grabs a sheet. Isis returns to the kitchen.

Perry I've got some tramadol for my back but it's in my caravan
I left everything
All my medication
I was holding on to that hedge for my life
I tell you, I was crying

Perry is crying. Anton is bringing lamps and candles over to Ripley.

Ripley Ruth, we're going to roll you on your side. (*To Anton.*) Would you help?

Anton makes to lift Ruth.

Ted I'll do that

Ripley No

Ted I said I'll do that

Ripley Keep out of my way

Ted stalks away, battle lines drawn. Anton helps Ripley. Dora lays a sheet over the chaise.

Perry I was praying and I don't believe in God

Fiske God's with us, Perry. He's here
I feel as if He's holding this house in His hand

Ripley (*to Dora*) Find me a sewing kit, darling

Anton Everything's okay, Ruth. It'll all be fine

Diana comes back with more bedding.

Ruth (*to Anton*) Where are we?

Anton Big house full of old stuff

Diana This is Burnt Marple. The village is named after this house

Ted Restoration. All will be restored

Diana I hope so

Isis enters. Diana goes back upstairs.

Isis There's no paracetamol – but this is my dad's hash

Ripley I'm going to give you some, Ruth

Ruth I don't take drugs

Ripley You'll need analgesics. (*To Isis.*) Boiling water, please

Isis It's an Aga. It's really slow

Isis returns to the kitchen.

Perry I thought I was a goner
If I hadn't caught that hedge
I was pulling it up by the roots

Ted (*turning his attention to Perry*) What's your name, mate?

Perry Perry

Ted Perry? That's pear cider – a fine old English name

Perry Are you staying here?

Ted No, I'm a refugee, just like you

Perry I'm not a refugee

Ted From the storm, no offence. Ted

Ted holds out his hand. Perry gingerly shakes. Ripley puts on surgical gloves.

Perry I cut my hand on the bushes, Ted
Fuck me, you're Ted Farrier

Ted That's right, my friend

Perry I've been on your website

Ted In the morning, Perry, we must have some chats

Ripley takes some flash photographs of Ruth's injury with her phone.

Why are you doing that?

Ripley I'm making a record of the injury. Is there a reason you object?

Ted I don't object. Seems gruesome and pointless

Ripley (*under her breath*) So do you

Dora returns with a sewing kit. She hands it to Ripley.

Thanks. Could you get me a light?

Diana comes down with quilts.

Diana I think this is everything we have

Isis enters with hot water. Fiske stands.

Fiske Dear Lord
You saved us from the might of the waters overflowing
You are our refuge and our fortress
In Your wings shall we trust
We fear not the terror by night
The arrow by day
Nor the wrack of destruction that wastes in the storm
Amen

Anton Amen

Ted I'd like to thank you, Diana, for sharing your home on the toughest of nights
In terrible circumstances for your family
You've welcomed us all
And it shows your exceptional grace
We're lucky, very lucky to have found you

Diana Thank you

Ripley I'm very sorry, Ruth, I have to see the base of the wound. This might hurt

44

Ruth screams in agony as Ripley examines her wound.

Diana If everyone's comfortable I might go up
I'm suddenly all done in.
Ripley, do you need anything else?

Ripley No, thank you

Ripley starts cleaning the wound.

Diana Isis, will you come to bed?

Isis I'm going to stay with Dad

Diana He doesn't need you, you should sleep

Isis I'm going to stay with Dad

Diana Dominic, would you like a room?

Fiske Better off here. Going to rest the old ticker. You're a marvel for taking us in

Perry I'll have a room

Diana I'm sure you're better where you are

Perry No I'm not; I'm sitting in wet

Diana There's a cloakroom through the kitchen

Perry For my cloak?

Diana It's a lavatory

Diana turns, to find Ted in her path. Isis regards them both.

Ted There must be something I can do for you

Diana considers him. She holds out a blanket.

Diana Goodnight

SCENE THREE

*Later. The rain is still intense, beginning to lessen as the
scene progresses. Isis is in the kitchen, sleeping, her head on
the table, next to Pete. Ted is looking at the accounts,
candlelit. Ruth is on the chaise. Ripley is stitching the
laceration on her back. Dora assists, holding a lamp. Perry
and Fiske are sleeping. Anton is near Ruth, under a blanket,
awake. Ruth cries out.*

Dora So what d'you do, Ruth, what's your job?

Ruth I'm a homemaker

Dora What, like an architect?

Ruth No, like a housewife. I used to lecture in History

Dora Seriously? I'm going to study it at uni

Ruth You should. It illuminates our path
      History is the onward journey of the human race

Ripley Look ahead and keep very still

Dora So what's your era?

Ruth My first book was on the Reign of Terror

Dora When the French guillotined all the rich? We should
do that again

Ruth You think so?

Dora One per cent of the population on this planet owns
over half its wealth. They should be made to give it up

Ripley By whom?

Dora The people

Ripley You mean us?

46

Dora Yes

Ripley And what force do we use to implement this change, which form of violence?

Dora There's no point talking to you

Ripley Why not?

Dora You're too reasonable. It's boring

In the kitchen, Isis wakes. She sees Ted.

Isis What are you doing?

Ted (*turning to her*) I'm watching over things, for your mother

Isis (*standing*) Get away from there

Ted We haven't been properly introduced –

Isis Leave our stuff alone

Ted I'm very sorry about your dad. My name's Ted

Isis I know

Ted Ted Farrier

Ted approaches her with his hand held out.

Isis (*points*)You can sleep in there

Ted I'd love to but I'm not tired. Is there a reason you won't shake my hand?

Isis I don't want you in here

Ted Goodnight then

Ted relents. He goes into the Great Hall. Anton has now fallen asleep.

Ruth How bad is it? Would I have bled to death?

Ripley (*glancing at Ted*) The real threat is infection. Tell us more about the Reign of Terror

Ruth The ruling elite had put themselves apart. So the people decapitated them. But it wasn't a victory. It led to chaos. When people are hungry, they need a vision; someone who'll take their anger and turn it into change. They need a leader. The French Revolution floundered until the rise of Napoleon; one extraordinary, dynamic man

Ripley He was a slaver

Dora Didn't he plunge the whole of Europe into war?

Ruth Wars are a part of our evolution
    Look what wars achieve
    Napoleon forced the British to find their strength
    We beat him – and for the next hundred and fifty years, Britain brought civilisation to the rest of the world

Dora What?

Ripley What do you mean by civilisation?

Ruth Us. I lie awake at night, grieving that this nation's come so low. We're desperate for a strong, benevolent leader with a vision of our greatness. Superior cultures need to protect themselves

Ripley Fuck off
    I need to keep steady, Ruth, or your back'll be a mess

Ruth Then we should talk about something else

Ripley No, I want Dora to hear what you think

Ruth My latest book is called *Lords of the Future*. You should read it

Ripley I don't think I will, thank you

Ruth Why not?

Ripley Because you're Ruth Getz

Dora Who's Ruth Getz?

Ripley Albion

Dora (*to Ripley*) She's Albion?

Ripley They all are, all three of them

Dora You know who she is and you're fixing her up?

Ripley That's what I do

Dora You gave her hash for her pain?

Ripley I've spent my life fixing up the weakest. And right now, Ruth, that's you

Ruth I'm not weak

Ripley The Lords of the Future mowed you down. They pushed you in the flood and walked away

Dora Did Ted Farrier slash you up?

Ruth He left his wife and family for me
We're two halves of one whole
Ted would never hurt me

Ted is satisfied with this. He climbs the stairs. He looks at the pictures of Diana and Pete. Ripley's needle goes into Ruth's flesh. Ruth moans in pain.

Ripley I need the light, darling

Dora Fuck's sake
So Ruth, I hear that Albion says women should give up their jobs for men?

Ted listens, on the staircase.

Ruth You can link the rise in divorce, abortion, male suicide and rape directly to women entering the workplace

Dora Oh my fuck, that's bollocks

Ripley You said it. You swear

Dora You're laying the blame for men's behaviour on women – what the fuck?

Ruth My life's improved tenfold since I gave up work
It doesn't mean we have no power
We're lionesses and shield maidens
And we know the ecstasy of surrender

Ripley You didn't give up work. I read you were sacked from your faculty for whitewashing genocides

Ruth You know all about me; I'm flattered. Historically, genocides are the natural order; part of what we do as a species, just as slavery is

Ted (*a warning*) Ruth

Ruth I want some water

Ted goes into the kitchen. Isis stands as he comes in. He gets water.

Ripley You're Jewish, aren't you?

Ruth No

Ripley I read that you were

Ruth I'm certainly not. But even if I was, there'd be a place for me in Albion

Ripley So you're multicultural fascists; what a broad appeal

Ruth We're not fascists or racists – and I can tell you're black, Judith, by your voice. In Albion, we choose to belong. Are you British, or not?

Ripley Oh my God, you're so frightening

Perry (*calling out in his sleep*) Nan

In the kitchen, Ted sips Ruth's water. Isis stands guard over Pete.

Ruth Ted will lead us to a better place. He's a great man

Ripley That's not what you said earlier. You asked for my protection

Ruth Lovers argue. I was in pain

Ripley This is a really deep wound; there's impact. Were you pushed?

Ted enters the Great Hall.

Ruth You know what it felt like? Like the flood itself got hold of me. Like the flood itself, in blackness and hatred, was bearing down on me, roaring down my neck

Ripley You're afraid of him

Ruth There's always an element of fear between a woman and a man

Ripley In abusive relationships, yes

Ted Here's your water, my love

Ruth Thank you

Ted puts the water in Ruth's hand. He kisses her and exits to the kitchen.

Dora Can I go now please?

Ripley Yes

Dora You should shake some salt on that

Ruth How aggressive you are

Dora goes to lie in a distant chair and pulls a quilt right up to her head.

Ripley You're the most violent woman I've ever heard speak

Ripley finishes. The rain stops.

Ruth Do you regret stitching me up?

Ripley No

Ruth How nobly professional

Ripley But you might get sepsis

Ripley goes into the kitchen. She stops short when she sees Ted. He's looking at Isis.

Ted The kind thing to do for your mother would be to move him off the table

Isis Don't touch him

Ted There must be a cold store. All these old places have larders. He can't stay here, can he, love?

Isis Fuck off

Ripley That's a very clear request

Ted goes through the Great Hall. He goes outside. Anton wakes.

Ripley You must be worn out
Why don't I keep vigil?

Isis You'll watch over him?

Ripley Yes. Go to bed

Isis Don't let me sleep long

Ripley I won't

Isis Don't let anything happen

Ripley I promise. Go and rest

Isis Thank you

Isis goes upstairs. Ripley photographs the burn on Pete's neck.
Anton comes to Ruth. He takes her hand.

Anton Ruth

Ruth Where is he?

Anton Outside

Ruth I provoked him to a rage
He didn't know I'd fall
He didn't see what was down there
I know he regrets it; I can feel his pain

Anton Not his pain; yours

Ruth He needs us, Anton. He needs us

Anton You know what I think?
I think there could be a thousand Teds
But there is only one of you

Ted comes back into the Great Hall. Anton kisses Ruth's hand and goes back to his chair.

Ted The rain's stopped

Anton pretends to be asleep. Ted walks through the space, looking at Diana's artefacts and clutter.
The moon comes out. Ted appreciates the ghostly light. He moves in it, almost like a dancer.

In the kitchen, Pete stirs. He sits up, bewildered. Concussed. Hungover. Sick in his guts. He gets off the table. He steadies himself. He doesn't see Ripley; she's sitting by the Aga in a deep sleep.

Pete exits, down the corridor to the cloakroom.

Act Two

*A few hours later. Dawn saturates the hall. Wind is
whipping the house.*

> *Ripley is sleeping in the kitchen.*

> *Fiske, Anton, Perry and Ruth are asleep in the Great
Hall.*

> *Dora is awake, watching Ted explore. He picks up a cane
and discovers it's a sword-stick.*

> *He brandishes it in the air. Then wakes Anton with the
tip. Anton startles.*

Ted Antique sword-stick
> From the days when men were always armed
> Check it out

He gives it to Anton. Anton regards it.

Look at this place
> Built out of the rubble of a civil war
> This brave manor holds the history of our nation
> Poised looking out to sea, protecting our shores
> Repelling invaders for centuries

Anton Yeah

Ted It's an Englishman's home
> Do you feel that?

Anton Yes

Ted Fuck conference suites, they could be anywhere
> We need a base, a sanctuary, a castle
> Chequers, the Berghof
> Even Stalin had his country house
> This manor

We could restore it
Honouring the wood and stone of our land

Anton You mean renovate it?

Ted This manor represents all that we're fighting for

Anton looks around. He doesn't see Ted's vision.

Anton Is it for sale?

Ted No. But I'll have it

Anton For Albion?

Ted It *is* Albion

Anton What do you mean?

Ted D'you have no vision? We're just beginning, Anton, we're ascendant. I can think in a place like this. I can invade. We've got five million in crowdfunding

Anton That's not what it's for, though

Ted It's to restore Britain

Anton Yes but that's not literal. You mean restore it for the people

Ted How long have you been in love with Ruth?

Anton How would I betray you like that, after everything you did for me?

Ted I like the way you return my question with a question. I taught you that

Anton I don't know what you think you saw. But I'm not that kind of man

Ted My anger's passed and I don't blame you
   Ruth is rare; she's a nonpareil
   D'you know what that means?

Anton No

Ted It's Shakespeare. 'Matchless'
Ruth herself taught me that.
Shall I tell you what I saw?
I saw her take your head in her hands like this

He takes Anton's head in his hands. Dora watches.

I saw her kiss you with such tenderness
An intimacy, moving to behold

Anton It was the anniversary of my mother's death
She said she'd lost her mother too
She asked if I would give her strength

Ted She doesn't need your strength
She isn't weak
She's as potent as that storm
She enthrals us with her courage
Seeming vulnerable in order to control.
I watch her operate on you
And I know that's what she did to me
She's beguiled us both

Anton Nothing happened
She's completely loyal to you
Ted, I owe you everything

Ted I had a go at you and it was wrong
You're my right hand

Anton Darren and Chris, I think they turned right
I went the wrong way

Ted No, Anton, it was right
We're meant to be here
This is meant to be

A back-slappy hug.

It makes a woman feel strong when she puts strife between men
Just watch yourself

Anton nods, affected. Ted moves away.

I'll go down to the car, get the case, breathe the air, see the lay of the land

Anton I'll come with you

Ted No. We'll be lords of this manor

Anton Cool

Ted When they wake up, be here
Let's show them who we are
This is an opportunity
Acts of chivalry and valour, natural leadership
The lady of the manor is going to need her knights

Ted takes his cane and goes out. Anton notices Dora.

Anton Hi
Did you sleep okay?

Dora No

Dora moves to the window.

Anton Funny old place this, isn't it?
What's your name?

Dora Isadora

Anton Like the explorer?

Dora Like my great-grandmother

Diana comes onto the landing, dressed in a satin dressing gown, her hair attractively tousled.

Diana Good morning

Anton Good morning

Diana Would you tell Mr Farrier I want him

Anton You've just missed him; he's gone out to the car

Diana Oh. When he returns, would you send him up?

Anton Is there anything I can help you with?

Diana No

Anton I was thinking we should make a rescue flag; unfurl it out the window, so if helicopters pass, they know there's people here

Diana Yes, quite right

Anton A white sheet with 'SOS' – for Ruth

Diana Very good. How is she?

Anton All stitched up

Diana She's engaged to Ted?

Anton Yes

Diana How long for?

Anton Three years

Diana Oh lovely. Do tell him to come up

Diana exits, upstairs. Dora is looking out of the window. Anton joins her.

Anton It's like the whole world is drowned out there
Like the zombies are coming, isn't it?

Dora I think the zombies are already here

Anton decides to let this go.

Anton So what d'you think about making a flag? We could do it with one of these sheets here

Dora Are you trying to make normal conversation?

Anton I'm planning for our rescue

Dora Someone needs to rescue you

Anton From what?

Dora (*pointing at Ruth*) She's not the blind one, is she?

Anton You don't know anything about me

Dora Then explain

Anton Is there any point? You're judging me already

Dora moves away.

Your mum's been great to Ruth

Dora She is great

Anton She reminds me of my mum a bit
My mum raised me by herself

Dora What does she think about you joining the Klan?

Anton She's dead
And this isn't the Klan; you've got it wrong
This is a good path
D'you mind me asking how old you are?

Dora Eighteen

Anton That's the age I was, when my mum died

Dora That's hard

Anton My dad, he was nowhere
Couldn't even find him.
I couldn't pay the rent, couldn't cope with the bills
And I was an adult, so I was evicted

Dora Wow

Anton I was uncontrollable for a while
Anyone who even looked at me odd would get it
I ended up in prison
By some miracle I got on the education wing and I began
to read
A man came in to give this talk
Said we could turn ourselves around
It was Ted
He said he'd been there

Talked about our anger
How it came from a part of us that's not at liberty.
He said we could all be better, truer men
If you transform yourself, you can transform the world.
Somehow those words went in.
I've seared them on my bones now
I wrote to Ted
And when they let me out, he sponsored me.
Ted and Ruth believed in me, when no one else was there

Dora I bet they made you feel like a prince

Anton Am I wasting my words?

Dora They went recruiting in jail. That's so cynical

Anton You're determined not to hear me

Dora Ted and Ruth gave you hope and in return, you're the poster boy for the Übermensch

Anton Even the fact that you know that word
I don't know that word – what is that –
What are you calling me?
You might as well be calling me gjsdfkshit
Because you're talking over my head
You're talking at me like I'm dumb

Dora It means super race. They think they're the super race and I don't understand / how someone like you

Anton You don't understand because you don't listen; one of those college girls with buoyant hair

Dora So tell me. Because I listen to that snaky woman Ruth and I just see genocide. Genocide and slave ships

Anton They found a Stone Age body in the Cheddar caves
They reproduced him from his genome
Skin darker than yours; bright blue eyes
A ten-thousand-year-old Briton
He was black

Dora Is that true?

Anton Yes. Black skin belongs here but we have to love this country with a proper zeal. This isn't about race

Dora Oh come on

Anton This is about poverty. Albion says refuse what you've been offered by the liberal elite. I refuse food banks and charity shops, evictions and job theft. I refuse crime and addiction. I refuse to be unwanted trash, like that fat bloke in the chair. Albion was the only voice that ever said to me you can play your part, you matter. You metropolitan liberals, you have no idea. My mum ate beans. We had nothing. She ate fucking beans. I won't be like that. I mean something now and she'd be proud of me

Dora If I joined, would I mean something?

Slow, intermittent taps from upstairs. Just audible.

Anton Of course you would
    You'd be more valued than you are now
    All the pressure that's on you –
    I bet you wake up every day, terrified you'll fail.
    Girls are expected to behave like men;
    And you're unsupported because men have lost their strength.
    You'll never have a proper home
    No time to nurture children
    You'll always be third best

Dora You're like a jihadi

Anton What did you say?

Dora They tell you their whole life to get you in their cause. That's their method. They make you sympathise

Anton What did you just call me?

Dora I think you've been brainwashed

Isis appears on the landing.

Anton Are you afraid of the future?

Dora Yes

Anton You don't have to be. All we want is to protect you

Dora Would you protect me, as you took away my rights?

Anton You have the right to be protected

Dora If you knew what I really was, you'd burn me as a witch

Isis (*on the landing*) Is he bothering you?

Dora I'm fine, thanks

Isis Can you hear that tapping?

They listen. Silence.

Whenever you talk about it, it stops. We've got a presence

Dora Seriously? Can I see it?

Isis It's incorporeal – so no. But I can show you where it chills

Dora climbs the stairs. Anton follows.

Not you

Anton remains at the foot of the stairs, frustrated. Dora and Isis exit. Perry and Fiske have woken.

Perry Still alive then, Vicar

Fiske It would appear so

Perry Us and the ducks

Fiske Yes, lovely weather for ducks

Perry I usually take my tablets first thing
But my medication's in my caravan

Fiske Oh dear

Perry I need it. I've got blood pressure and issues

Fiske We'll have to put your medication on a list of things
to do

Perry It's for kidney function and antidepressants.
Sometimes, I get bad

Fiske Diana lost her husband last night so I'm afraid her
needs come first

Perry Lost him where?

Fiske He died, Perry

Perry But I knew him

Fiske Yes

Perry He used to talk to me
He'd come down and chew the fat
Did he drown?

Fiske No

Perry I bet loads of people pegged it in that flood
I bet there's corpses bobbing everywhere
Tangled up in trees like dead pterodactyls,
Faces stuck to windscreens, trapped in cars
Eyes like Halloween creme eggs

Fiske I sincerely hope not

Perry My hands are cut, look, where I clung on

Fiske Oh golly

Perry I was going to be sucked out to sea
I'd be bloating up by now, all white and green
Cheeks nipped by fish lips, sinking down
And bioluminescent eels would feast on me

Fiske It didn't happen, Perry

Perry My caravan. I've lost everything

Perry starts to cry. Anton goes into the kitchen.

Fiske But we rescued you
That's the important thing
You're all right

Perry Even my photos
My nan
She'll have been snuffed out
Just a blur on a wet piece of paper now
My telly, my speakers, my laptop; all pissed on

Fiske I'm sure it's the same at the rectory
I managed to get my rare books upstairs but
I couldn't save my globe

Perry How can you believe in God when this happens?
Why's he doing this?

Fiske Well it's arguable
Perry, isn't it
That we're doing it

Perry No we're not; I didn't do this

Fiske We're heating the Earth's atmosphere and weather
systems are changing in response

Perry That's not true though. They've proven that's not true

Fiske Who has?

Perry Scientists

*Anton pours a glass of water. He stands for a moment,
looking at Ripley.*

Fiske All the major scientific institutions in the world are
saying that we're rapidly heating the planet and it's having
a major effect on all kinds of things

Perry So what's God's plan? How's he going to sort it out?

Fiske I'm not sure He can. I think it's up to us

Perry What's the point of him then? He must have a plan. What's his plan with this flood upending my trailer and wrecking my tech? What's his plan automating the tills at Sainsbury's so I lost my job? I used to help people with their shopping, now I'm worth less than a sodding machine

Anton puts a blanket over the sleeping Ripley. He sees the shroud on the table, finds a marker pen and writes 'SOS' on it.

Fiske Sometimes God's plan is greater than we can see. But these hurdles in our lives, these awful obstacles that we face, may ultimately lead us to a better place

Perry How?

Fiske Well for example, when my wife found out I was gay, my world collapsed; I thought my life was over. I was suicidal and I couldn't understand how God –

Perry I'm not gay

Fiske No, I'm not suggesting

Perry I'm not gay

Fiske No but I was going to say that I had been lying to myself and to my wife

Perry I've got nothing against gays

Fiske I'm just using it as an example, Perry. I was living a lie and God

Perry I'm all about live and let live, me

Fiske What I'm saying is that God helped me find my true self by taking away the things I held dear

Perry I know my true self already

Fiske I'm saying that out of adversity great things can come

Ted enters, limping, with his cane. He has a briefcase,
which he places by Ruth.

Maybe that's what God intends with this climate emergency
    If we can rise to it, it may be our finest hour

Ted Our finest hour
    The whole shape of the coast's gone
    Our land's been violated by the sea
    This is truly the battle for Britain

Perry Wow

Ted There's a stink to that flood; salt, iron, muck
    The water's alive; you can feel the malice
    You wade into the flow and it's a powerful enemy.
    We have to pit ourselves against it
    Trees uprooted, fish dead in hedgerows
    Even the light . . . The sky looks green.
    These are the battle-moves of chaos
    And it must be bested. Bested and subdued

Fiske Are you suggesting that we fight nature?

Perry I was battling for my life

Fiske We're here on Earth to serve nature

Ted We've got dominion though, haven't we, Rev?
    God gave us dominion

Fiske God and nature are one and the same

Ted I won't argue with your collar, Rev
    But on a day like this we should all pull together

Fiske I'm simply saying that when we oppose creation, we
oppose God

Ted No place for argument and strife
    Perry, we were going to have some chats

Perry Yeah

Ted So you're a native of these parts?

Perry Born and bred

Ted Salt of the earth

Perry I was telling the vicar I lost my job at Sainsbury's

Ted Well that's not right, is it?

Perry No

Fiske If you'll excuse me. Nature calls

Fiske goes upstairs. Ruth wakes.

Perry I feel a bit shy talking to you

Ted Why?

Perry Cos you're like not exactly famous but

Ted We're outlaws, Perry, we're notorious
Hounded by those who don't like our truth
And I want to hear about this job you lost

Perry They replaced me with self-service scanners

Ted Who's 'they'?

Perry The management

Ted Don't they have a name?

Perry Gurpreet

Ted Did Gurpreet decide who stayed and who went?

Perry There was no fairness in it. It should've been if you'd served longest – but this girl, Irenka, she'd only been there a year. Basically, if you sucked up to Gurpreet, you got to stay. I couldn't be arsed; I didn't like her. She basically said I was lazy. I said I'm not fucking lazy, I can't stack shelves cos I've got bad joints. I've got a heart condition; what d'you want me to do?

Ted So Irenka and Gurpreet kept their jobs while you, a fine, upstanding Englishman were pushed out?

Perry Yeah

Ted How does that make you feel?

Perry Really shit. I sat in that caravan, I tell you. I boiled

Ted Makes me feel really shit too. You heard of visualisation techniques?

Perry Maybe

Ted You should imagine you've got Gurpreet in a chair in front of you

Perry Now?

Ted Why not? What would you like to say?

Perry She'd take me to a tribunal

Ted Why?

Perry She'd say I'm sexist or racist. They all do

Ted Put a gag on her
Visualise her gagged
Now say what you think

Ruth (*a warning*) Ted

Ted It's all right, Perry understands me; he's one of us

Perry I've gagged her

Ted Tell her what you think. Say it aloud

Perry Gurpreet, you're a fucking cow

Ted No one'll hear but me and Ruth. And we agree with you

Perry You're a nasty, ugly bitch

Ted What kind?

Perry A fucking slag Paki

Ted How d'you feel now?

Perry Better
  She's a cunt, Ted

Ted Steady on, mate, let's respect Ruth

Perry Oh I'm sorry

Ted D'you know what I see when I look at you?

Perry Don't

Ted Potential

Perry I know exactly what you see

Ted That's just your cocoon. You'll shake that off. One day, you're going to emerge transformed – like an Oleander Hawk. Do you know what that is?

Perry No

Ted One of the most amazing moths in the world. It lives on the nectar of poisonous flowers

Perry Wow. I'm an Oleander Hawk

Ted There's people here who need our help
  The bereaved, that old vicar, two young girls –

Ruth I need you

Ted We need to show these people our leadership. If I call on you, will you step up?

Perry Yeah

Ted Good man, good man

Perry But I need my medication. I've got blood pressure and diabetes

Fiske comes down the stairs.

69

Fiske I'm going to get my gear on, Perry, then we'll see about your medication

Ruth Ted, someone needs to go out to the car

Ted Been there. Done it. Your case is by your side

Ruth feels for her case. Its presence comforts her.

Ruth Thank you

Ted Sit on it and guard it like a little shrew

Ruth Ted, we need to talk

Ted What about?

Ruth Come to me

Ted You told that doctor not to let me near you
So I'll stay well away

Anton enters with the shroud. Fiske exits outside.

Anton I made this. (*To Ruth.*) It's a massive banner. It says 'SOS'

Ruth You're a hero, Anton

Anton (*to Ted*) The lady wants to see you

Ted Where is she?

Anton She said to send you up

Ted Why didn't you tell me?

Ted climbs the stairs. He is halfway up when Isis and Dora come onto the landing.

Isis No

Ted No what?

Isis You can't come up

Ted Good morning. Your mother invited me

Isis No she didn't

Dora Actually, she did

Isis Why?

Ted Let's ask her, shall we?

Isis No

Ted climbs another couple of steps. Isis doesn't move.

Ted What's your name?

Isis Isis

Ted Pretty memorable name. Some sort of Roman goddess, aren't you, like Diana?

Dora She's a terrorist organisation

Isis I'm Egyptian

Ted What are you the goddess of, Isis?

Isis I'm the universal female
Water goddess, earth goddess, corn goddess, star goddess
Queen of the underworld
I gave birth to Heaven and Earth
I made Osiris a penis when he'd lost his own

Dora Right

Isis I care for widows and orphans,
Seek justice for the poor
And I keep the god of war on my knee, like a baby

Diana appears, stylishly dressed.

Diana (*to Ted*) Oh good, you're here. I need you to come to the barn with me. I have to face what's happened

Ted Of course. Anything

Isis Why are you asking him? I'm here; it's my barn

Diana There's a drowned sheep caught up in front of it. I thought it might upset you

Ted I'll be waiting outside

Diana Take the boots by the door

Isis You can't give him Dad's boots

Diana Isis, your dad doesn't need them any more

Ted Perfect fit

Ted goes outside, with Pete's boots.

Isis What are you doing?

Diana I'm mitigating a catastrophe

Isis Look at you – all made-up, your best cashmere on

Diana Be in no doubt of our desperate situation. That man can help us

Isis My father has just died

Diana We're about to lose this house and I think he's been sent by fate

Isis Do you know what he is? He's the far right

Diana No he's not, I got no sense of that

Isis Get me a bucket; you think he's hot

Diana I do not. But he's dynamic and we need a man of action

Isis Are you going to fuck him, Mum?

Diana Don't you dare stand in judgement over me
      I'm alive and kicking and I won't die just because my husband has

Isis Can't you be single, even for a day?
      What's so bad about being alone?

Diana You're solitary by nature
  I tried and tried to get you friends when you were small;
  You could never keep them
  That man could change our lives

Diana goes downstairs and outside.

Dora Wow

Isis I'm used to it

Anton I need to get upstairs to hang this from a window?

Isis Where did you get that?

Anton It was on the kitchen table

Isis Are you fucking joking?

Isis and Dora hurry into the kitchen.

Where's my dad?
  Where is he?

Ripley Oh my God

Isis Dad
  DAD

SCENE TWO

*In the kitchen, Ted, Diana, Isis, Dora, Anton, Fiske and
Ripley have gathered around the table.*
  *In the Great Hall, Ruth is sitting up on the chaise,
sorting the contents of her briefcase. She can sense
something.*

Ripley He can't have been dead

Diana I put my ear to his chest
  We checked his pulse
  There was no breath

Isis I couldn't feel any, but

Diana You said he was dead
  We lifted him up and dragged him
  He was a corpse
  It nearly killed us to get him on the table
  (*To Ripley.*) You examined him

Ripley I didn't actually touch him

Ruth Ted

Ripley I'd hardly got past the burn on his neck before

Diana He was as dead as a doornail

Isis (*to Ted*) Did you move him?

Ted No, I did not

Isis What have you done with my fucking dad?

  We hear tapping. Perry enters the kitchen from the back corridor.

Perry There's a vomit in the sink
  And a rank mess in your toilet

Isis Oh my God

Perry I didn't do it

Isis Dad
  Dad

  Ripley, Isis and Dora immediately exit down the back corridor. Diana takes the difficult news.

Ruth Ted, if you're there, just tell me

Fiske Diana, it's extraordinary
  He might be alive

Ted There's these states of deep unconsciousness
  Drugs, booze, concussion shut him down

Diana I'm really shocked

Ted We'll find him

Anton Yeah, don't worry

Ruth Don't do this, Ted. I hate this game

Isis returns with Ripley and Dora. She immediately starts dressing for outside.

Isis He must be alive

Ripley The back door's open. He might have gone out

Isis I'm going to find him

Dora We'll come with you

Ripley and Dora begin to get ready.

Diana Isis, don't put yourself in danger. If the water's deep –

Isis You'd love him to be dead, wouldn't you?

Diana How could you say that?

Ted Gents, why don't we search outside?

Anton Sure

Ted Girls, you stay indoors and search the house

Isis Why don't you clean our toilet, Ted?

Ted I would gladly but I have a task

Isis We need you to do it

Diana No we don't

Isis It's the toughest task that no one wants. Surely that's the one for the leader

Diana He's our guest

Isis I want Ted to mop my father's shit up

Wind is beginning to whip around the house.

Fiske I'll clean your loo, my dear friends

Isis No

Fiske I know you're upset but we must pull together
God may have given us a miracle

Isis (*to Fiske, pointing at Ted*) He's a far-right fascist

Ted Anton, am I a far-right fascist?

Anton No, mate

Dora (*to Anton*) That's why he has you. That's what he's
trained you to say

Ripley He leads Albion

Fiske Well I'm very disappointed, Ted

Isis Let's go

*Isis slams her way out through the Great Hall. Dora and
Ripley follow.*

Perry I need my medication. If I don't get it I'm in massive
trouble

Fiske (*to Ted*) Rescue will come. And in the time we have
together, I'm going to sway you from this dreadful path

Ted I'll look forward to that but right now, there's a man
lost and Perry needs his pills

Perry You're too good, Ted

Ruth Who's there?

Ripley It's Ripley

Ruth There are spiders in my dressing

Ripley (*to Dora*) I'd better check on her. Please be careful

Dora We will

Ripley I'm so sorry I can't get you home

Dora It's all right. It's not as boring as I thought

Dora and Isis go. Ted, Anton and Fiske are getting ready.

Ted Which caravan's yours, mate?

Perry It's got a green door, like the Shakin' Stevens song. Everything I need's in a plastic tub above the sink

Diana The well
Dominic – Pete jumped down it once, for a dare
At one of our parties – I don't want Isis finding him

Fiske Oh Lord

Anton Where is it?

Fiske Follow me

Fiske and Anton go. Diana grabs her coat.

Perry What should I do? I can't go outside. I've got bad joints

Diana Perhaps you'd clean the cloakroom

Perry Are you joking?

Diana No

Ted It's the toughest job; the one for a leader. I'm calling on you, Perry

Perry Like the speed of light

Perry goes. Diana is about to exit after Anton and Fiske. Ted holds her back.

Ted Don't go. I need you

Diana What for?

Ted To shine on me like the rising moon
But for starters, my ankle's agony

That nurse won't come near me
You must have something

Diana Sit

Ted Thank you

Diana finds a bandage.

So what went down with your husband?
   I mean forgive me but you don't seem over-thrilled at the thought that he's alive

Diana We were like two magnets that used to stick together and then somehow we turned ourselves around

Ted Did he fall or did you push him?

*Diana doesn't answer. She tapes Ted's foot in silence.
Ripley enters.*

Ripley I've used the only dressing. Have you got any tampons or sanitary towels? They're near sterile

Diana Oh – up the back stairs and straight in front of you. Mirror cabinet

Ripley goes.

My daughter's very upset

Ted She's had a massive shock

Diana Why does she hate you? I'm at a disadvantage, having never heard of you. What aren't you telling me?

Ted I'd lay every card in my dog-eared pack in front of you
   What do you want to know?

Diana She says you're a fascist

Ted I don't know what that means

Diana Would you send the weakest to the wall and push them if they don't go fast enough?

Ted Why send them to the wall, when they can clean your toilet?

Ripley walks through with tampons. She gets salt and hot water.

I won't hide anything from you.
  People don't like me because I acknowledge the degree
  The natural degree between us all, the grade.
  Some of us are more evolved, that's all

Ripley exits, disgusted.

Do you disagree with me?

Diana Yes. Some people are held back by things they can't help and as a society we should try to –

Ted That's not what you believe, that's what you say
  What you know to be true is that most people are boring.
  You've known all your life that you're better and more beautiful
  That's what you said to me last night

Diana It's not

Ted Degree is not to do with class or even culture. It's innate
  I help people find their proper place.
  There's a natural degree among the nations too
  The British could be vanguard, everywhere

Diana You'll never rule
  You'll never be elected

Ted Don't be so sure. I'm pulling the centre towards me

Diana What does that mean?

Ted It's moving right in my direction
  When it reaches me I'll step across

Diana You're all just people who want power

Ted I think the truth makes you uncomfortable
You want power too
You and me, we're leaders

Perry returns.

Perry I put bleach on and I flushed. That's as far as I'm going

Ted Perry, tell Diana what we're all about

Perry He's going to bring back jobs and smash the elite
He's giving us our self-respect
Britain needs its lions again
And you're going to hear me roar

Ted Nicely put. Crucial task, mate. Check on Ruth. Make sure that nurse is doing her job

Perry Faster than broadband

Perry exits to the Great Hall. He stands and watches as Ripley cleans Ruth's wound.

Ted Perry's life will improve in Albion

Diana It'd improve more if he went on a diet

Ted I'm glad you're not easy to impress. I love that

Diana Are you what my daughter says?

Ted I'm not a Nazi or a racist
I'm sorry she's angry
She's a great girl but
I get this all the time
People won't engage in a debate
Their prejudice nails me

Diana What to?

Diana has finished taping him up. Ted stands on the foot to test it.

Ted The radical statesman starts by being the outcast
Until his vision ignites
Then that vision makes him right

Diana Is there money in it?

Ted Yes

Diana Then you're a salesman peddling goods

Ted This is my faith

Diana No, you're in it for what you can get

Ted is poised for contact.

Ted What can I get?

Pause.

Diana I saw a door opening
I felt a weight lift
But I'm not free

Ted I can help you

Diana How?

Ted He's brought you down so low. He had all this and he pissed it up the wall. I'd have pushed him down the stairs for leading you this dance

Diana He turned on me
He said he would destroy my house

Ted Do you want it to be over?

She nods.

Say it. Tell me

Diana I want the struggle to be over

Ted I'll find him

Diana No, no
Don't do anything

Ted You deserve to be saved
If you pushed him, I will keep your secret

Diana I don't want him hurt

Ted You want a future. Say it

Diana Yes

They snog. Their passion escalates. Isis and Dora enter by the back door. Isis pulls Dora out again. In the hall, Ripley is cleaning Ruth's wound.

Ruth I felt someone, watching me

Ripley They say all these old places are haunted

Ruth Ted does that but only in fun. He creeps up

Ripley That's fun for you, is it?

Ruth Where is he?

Ripley In the kitchen, with the lady of the house

Ted You are
The centre

Diana Oh my God

Ripley What caused this wound?

Ruth We were arguing

Ripley About what?

Ripley puts her phone on video record. She places it where it can pick up Ruth.

Ruth We were by the car and I was provoking him

Ripley Provoking him how?

Diana comes up for air.

Diana Don't. Someone'll see

Ted Say 'Don't' again

Diana Don't

Ted Louder

Diana Don't

Ruth I didn't want to get back in the car. I was scared

Ted and Diana separate as Perry arrives in the kitchen.

Perry She's filming on her phone, trying to get Ruth to say stuff

Ted You're a diamond, Perry

Ruth The water was swirling
I was shouting at him, saying 'Don't leave me'
He called me stuff and I swore back

Ripley What did he do?

Ted goes into the Great Hall. Diana can't collect herself. She leaves through the back door.

Ruth Maybe I was unreasonable
But it came out of nowhere, this (shove) –

Ted What's going on?

Ripley Ruth's right. You do creep around

Ted Did you know this woman was filming you?

Ruth She's
Taking advantage of my blindness

Ted Give me that phone

Ripley No way

Ted makes a sudden grab for the phone. Ripley holds on to it. They struggle for possession.

Ted I can see your agenda

Ripley Get off –

Ted So this can go online?

Ripley Don't give me ideas

Ted Online, with a host of lies?

Ripley Get off me –

He assaults; she resists.

Ted Twisting events to destroy a man's life?

Ripley stamps on Ted's injured ankle. He cries out. Perry comes to the door, watching.

Bitch

Ruth I'd never talk to that feminist scum

Ted takes the phone, shoving Ripley across the room. She falls to the floor, shocked.

Ted Every day – goaded and attacked. Lampooned, spat upon, lied about – you people are fucking Pharisees

Ted goes outside with Ripley's phone. Fiske and Anton come into the kitchen with Diana.

Diana I've always dreaded that well

Fiske It's flooded. Anton was most thorough

Anton I climbed down the ladder; reached into the water

Fiske You can cross it off your list of worries

A slow tapping from upstairs. Ripley is looking out of the window; Perry still watching.

Ruth You shouldn't have tricked me

Diana My grandfather found human bones down there
A woman, dating from the Civil War

Ripley I treat women like you every day
Who lie about their bruises and their broken bones

Diana Maybe she was murdered
Maybe she was raped

Ruth I'm not a victim

Ripley Nor am I

Diana Maybe she was burning and she threw herself in

Fiske Poor soul

Ted walks through the Great Hall and into the kitchen.

Ripley Nobody does that to me and walks away

Ted Silly cow, you dropped your phone in the water

Ted reaches the kitchen.

Fear not, Perry, I'm going through that green door

He passes Diana.

Your struggle will end. Anton, outbuildings

Anton Right you are

Ted continues on and out through the back door.

Stay and get your breath back, Rev

Fiske No; we're going to have a hard talk, young man
You've got some awfully misguided views
My father served in Germany and he saw first hand the
horror of supremacist ideas

Anton and Fiske exit. Ripley enters the kitchen.

Ripley Diana, I need to warn you, about Ted

Diana Why?

Ripley He's just assaulted me

Diana What are you talking about?

Ruth is making her way towards the kitchen.

Ripley He got hold of me and grabbed my phone
He fought me for it and he's thrown it in the flood

Diana Why would he do that?

Ripley I was filming Ruth, trying to get her to speak. Ted pushed me to the ground

Diana is genuinely disturbed.

Diana That's very bad of him. It's very bad

Ripley I need your support

Diana Of course. I don't understand. Why would he do that?

Ruth enters the kitchen, aided by Perry.

Ripley He's a violent man. Ruth was about to confide in me

Ruth No I wasn't

Diana Ripley says that Ted assaulted her

Ruth Of course he didn't

Ripley Oh how predictable

Diana She says he knocked her to the ground and took her phone

Ruth That's absolutely scandalous. How dare she?

Ripley You're a contrarian by nature, aren't you, Ruth?

Ruth You're using my injury to malign Ted. He's done nothing

Ripley Tell the truth, for God's sake

Ruth We get this all the time; people abuse us, they make death threats; you're trying to fabricate an assault

Ripley I'm pressing charges

Ruth He's my lover and my better half and I'll fight to protect him tooth and nail
Your word against mine and I saw nothing
I need the bathroom

Diana Let me show you

Ruth I'd rather you didn't touch me please

Diana As you wish

Ruth None of this is as I wish

Perry Let me

Perry assists Ruth.

Ripley He's tired of you
It's in his face, every time he looks at you.
The glamour of your intellect's worn off.
He is and will be Ruthless

Ripley puts a knife in Ruth's hand.

Protect yourself. One day you'll need it
And Diana, WAKE UP

Ripley exits into the Great Hall. She tries to collect herself.

Ruth Ted would never hurt me

Perry He's got you fighting over him
I wish I was like that

Diana I want you people out of my house

Perry Well we're not going, are we?

Ruth takes up the knife, point facing Diana.

Ruth I'll keep this to remind me to fight for my beliefs.
I believe in my man

Fiske enters.

Fiske My light's out of charge. The garages are very dark

Perry Shall I take you to the toilet?

Ruth Thank you, Perry. You're very sweet and kind

Perry and Ruth exit.

Diana I told them to get out

Fiske Oh dear

Diana I'm not a good person

Fiske No one is

Diana Some of us are dreadful and horrible and mean

Fiske I don't think you are

Diana I'm even cruel to Isis
I said she had no friends – but nor do I
I'm not liked
I don't know how to love – I'm vain and selfish

Fiske It's hard to sustain love until you love yourself
Love forgives our flaws

Diana If by love you mean God, you can stop it right now

Fiske I'm just speaking as a friend. Michael was my first
true friend and he came very late in life

Diana I'm falling off a cliff
If the devil came along and said here's your house and
land restored, your debts paid, I'd put on my best dress and
dance for him

Fiske Diana
Adversity is a beginning, not an end

Pause.

88

Diana The back stairs. Pete might have gone up

Fiske Shall I come with you?

Diana No. Keep searching outside. There's a storm lantern in the game larder

Diana exits. Fiske exits. Dora and Isis enter the Great Hall. Isis makes straight for the stairs.

Isis He has to be somewhere
I know he's alive

Dora Slow down, get your breath back

Ripley Dora

Dora What is it?

Ripley Ted

Dora Mum – what did he do?

Ripley I'm okay

Dora Jesus, you're crying

Ripley He pushed me down

Dora Oh my fuck

Ripley He took my phone. It's a shock reaction, I'm fine

Dora No, no

Dora holds Ripley.

Isis I'm throwing them out – they're not staying in this house

Ripley They're dangerous – don't – don't do anything yet

Dora Let's go
The water's going down
We could wade through
Isis, come with us

Isis I can't leave my dad

Ripley I'm not running away

Dora Have you got proof?

Ripley Ruth will lie. It's my word against his

Dora I want to kill him

Ripley Don't do anything rash – d'you understand?

Dora As far as I'm concerned, it's war

Ripley We can be cleverer than that
They're unstable
Let's bide our time and maybe something will break
Keep looking for your dad and I'll find Dominic

Ripley goes out.

Isis On my survival course they said our generation will see war. Catastrophe is coming

Dora We'll have war because of white, hormonal men. Their testosterone is gonna kill the world

Isis The Amazon's on fire, the ocean can't sustain life –
We're the virus and the Earth is the host
She has to kill us off, in order to survive
We're destroying everything

Dora Isis, you've been on your own too much

Isis I've learnt to make fire and natural penicillin
I can shoot a rifle, skin a rabbit
I planted nut trees to sustain us through the winter
They'll die in this
Look at it out there
Look at Ted
People will destroy themselves

Dora I'm not saying that it's not a struggle
It's a massive struggle every day but
Don't you think that Ted's a dinosaur?

He's a like relic from a dying age
The future could go someplace else
You could leave here

Isis I don't know how to live
I'm twenty and I'm still at home
I pretend every day but I don't know how to live

Dora suddenly kisses her. It's a revelation to Isis and a glory to them both.

Dora We've got to do something

Isis wipes her eyes. She breathes deeply.

Isis Let's kill Ted

Dora No . . .

She sees Ted's briefcase. She takes it.

Let's fuck him up

Isis and Dora and exit upstairs, carrying the briefcase.

Act Three

Ripley enters the Great Hall, with Fiske.

Fiske It's monstrous
Judith, I'm so sorry
This was your weekend away in our lovely village

Ripley I know; I thought A&E was violent and stressful

Fiske I'd hoped Ted could be reasoned with

Ripley You can't reason with the far right
They're blazing with a flame of certainty

Fiske That young chap Anton is breaking my heart. With some forceful discourse, don't you think we could change his mind?

Ripley What forceful discourse would you suggest?

Fiske He's thoughtful; I think there's hope for him. I'm trying to plant a seed

Ripley He's in love with Ruth

Fiske Is he?

Ripley They've got him, lock, stock and barrel
They've got a natural fan in Perry. And Diana

Fiske She'll have no truck with them, believe me

Ripley I think she's happily seduced

Fiske No, no, Diana's not what you think
Pete was Labour, through and through
She was always a rebel

Supercool you know
Height of fashion when she married Pete

Ripley Maybe Ted's the height of fashion now

Fiske We get them in the church too
People peddling supremacy
Bigots, without an ounce of doubt.
Doubt lights the way in my book
It holds things up to proper scrutiny

Ripley Even faith?

During the following Diana enters. She sits at the top of the stairs, downcast. She begins to listen.

Fiske Yes, we have to question God. I've had terrible moments of doubt.
I pull apart the Bible all the time. Why did God give us dominion, dominion over everything that moveth on the earth? He must have foreseen what it would do

A bolt of lightning far away.

Our whole history's one of dominion, and one begins to fear –
I worry that love is puny by comparison

Anton enters.

Anton Where's Ruth?

Ripley I don't care

Anton I've searched round the back
A dead cat but nothing else.
I'll go and help Ted

Ripley You know he hurt Ruth, you know that

Anton It was pitch dark on that lane. No one could see; it was an accident

Ripley You sad, lost boy, they've tied you up in lies

Anton Don't patronise me

Ripley You're clinging to the Supermen
Holding on to the Lords of the Future
Hoping they won't notice that you don't belong

Anton This country's plagued by those who don't belong
Terrorists who'd bomb your daughter at a concert
Or mow you down in trucks
I'm order, safety, I'm protecting you
I am proud of who I am

Ripley The biggest threat to freedom that we face is you

Anton Freedom's what I fight for

Ripley Oh go and get a proper job

Anton I belong with Albion, I'm one of them.
I'm not clinging to the Supermen – I am the Supermen

Fiske Anton, think. What unites us all?

Ripley Come and work with me in A&E
Shadow me for just a day
You'd see survival isn't of the fittest
That's such a clever, nasty lie
Human beings survive because we're so connected
We're a social species; that's our strength
It's not power and self-interest
We listen and collaborate
We make bonds and look after one another
I spend my days with an amazing team
Fighting death and trauma –
With the old, the injured, the ill, the vulnerable –
People – in our difference, we are all the same
I see extraordinary strength and so much love
Ted is puny by comparison

Anton is affected.

Fiske Ted assaulted Ripley

Anton Why?

Ripley You'd better go and ask him

Fiske I can tell you categorically, he's going to pay the price

Anton exits. Diana exits, upstairs.

Ripley D'you think it's possible we washed up here for a reason?

Fiske I think we should confront Ted
Let's poke a stick into the hornets' nest
I'm rather sick with dread but back me up
We're going to make a citizens's arrest

Ripley laughs.

Ripley Does that make us the law?

Fiske Yes

Ripley But we don't have any power. We can't hold him

Fiske But when this is over, it's a mark against him and it carries weight. He has to answer to the police

Ripley You think the police are public servants, don't you?

Fiske Well of course

Ripley From where I stand, it's not that clear cut
There's plenty of the police agree with Ted

Fiske We must insist upon the rule of law. He assaulted you

Ripley Look – that window in the barn. There's someone there

Fiske Yes. Pete

Ripley and Fiske exit as Ruth and Perry return from the kitchen. Perry sits Ruth by the fire.

Ruth It's very cold. Are you cold?

Perry I'll build up the fire. I'm going to sit you back on the sofa. There's a blanket here

Ruth Thank you. Would you pass me my briefcase, please?

Perry What briefcase?

Ruth The briefcase

Perry There's nothing here, nothing

Ruth panics.

Ruth They can't have
　　　Ted must have hidden it
　　　They can't have stolen it
　　　We have to find that case

Perry What's in there?

Ruth Take my hand. I want to trust you with the future

Perry takes Ruth's hand. Diana comes onto the landing.

In the Middle Ages, our leaders sent nine crusades against an evil, invading Islam. Because of those crusades, Europe stayed pure for a thousand years. Now Islam's here. We've let it in, to bomb our cities and abuse our children. It's time for us to rise again. We and others like us are conceiving a Tenth Crusade. We need knights, willing to fight for a Britain that's strong and true

Perry Has your briefcase got your plans and that?

Ruth It can't fall into the wrong hands

Perry Oh my God, it's like James Bond
　　　I'm going to find it, Ruth
　　　Because if someone's taken it, that's disgusting
　　　That is stealing off the blind

Diana walks down the stairs.

Shhh. It's her

Diana puts on a once-smart Barbour jacket. She grabs some binoculars.

Ruth There's people here who'd like to cast me out into the flood

Perry How could they?

Diana Ted told me he was pulling the centre towards him and when it reached him he would step across. What does that mean? Does it mean he's going to leave your party and stand for the Conservatives?

Ruth If I wasn't in your house I'd say exactly what I think of you

Diana I think the far-right doggerel is yours, not his. He's an opportunist, isn't he?

Ruth You don't know anything about him

Diana I'm learning very fast

Diana exits.

Perry I bet she was boiling a cauldron in that storm

Ruth fails to control her distress.

Hey, come on, have you been peeling onions? That's what my nan used to say whenever I came in crying. She used to give me biscuits and she'd try to make me laugh. She'd do farts and blame them on me

Ruth Where was your mother?

Perry She had issues; she wasn't much around

Ruth My mother stuck it out until I was twelve. Then she got a job in Frankfurt. She was a chemistry professor. I think she couldn't wait to get away from me

Perry Fucking hell

Ruth My father said we must use our wounds to give us fortitude. Your mother's 'issues' didn't break you, Perry. You've overcome. And I'm not crying

Perry It's fantastic, Ruth, to be with you
    To listen to you say amazing things
    No one ever talks to me like this

Isis and Dora come downstairs. Thunder and lightning from outside.

Ruth You should come to one of our rallies
    There's such a thrilling atmosphere
    Men come to me and say 'I feel like I've spoken,
    Spoken for the first time'

Perry D'you feel you're part of something
    Like a band of brothers in World War Two?

Ruth That's exactly how it feels
    We're fighting for the soul of our country
    Just like they were then

Perry What about girls? Are there lots of girls?

Isis pulls Dora into a kiss.

Ruth That's one of the things you could help us with. We need to recruit more women.
    There are so many women looking for love. I'd say to them all, 'Come to a far-right rally.' White women don't have a sisterhood, like black women. They're alone and unhappy and they don't respect their men

Perry That's cos of feminism, isn't it

Ruth Absolutely. It's made us feel it's shameful to surrender to our heroes

Dora picks up the rifle. She pretends it's a machine gun and mimes firing at Ruth. Isis finds it hilarious. She picks up the other gun.

Perry I'm not a hero. Women don't like me

Ruth I'm sure they do, you're a lovely guy

Perry You're only saying that because you can't see me

Ruth I'm saying it because it's true

The girls are both giggling. Diana comes inside; sees them with the guns.

Diana What are you doing?

Perry Fucking hell

Isis I'm playing with my friend

Diana What game is that?

Dora Girl on girl with guns

Diana takes the rifle from Isis and puts it away.

Diana You're frightening me

Isis We're the least frightening people here

Perry They were pointing guns at us, Ruth

Ted enters, singing in the style of Shakin' Stevens. He has a bag of medication. One by one he throws the packs and bottles to Perry, singing lines from 'Green Door', with Perry supplying the chorus. During this, Anton enters, closing the door behind him.

Perry Fucking hell, you're a prince

Ruth Ted

Ted I'm going to be straight with you, Perry
There's a lot of damage
But your iPad has survived

Ted takes an iPad out of his waistband and gives it to Perry.

Perry My iPad. You're a fucking god

Ruth Ted

Ted It's otherworldly down there
  Feels sort of dreamlike doesn't it, Anton?

Anton No

Ted (*to Diana*) I searched everywhere; found nothing

Ruth Ted

Ted Fierce current, roaring everything out to sea
  Rain's coming in like rods
  Back to this haven not a moment too soon

Diana Did you hurt Ripley?

Ruth Our briefcase has gone

Diana Did you hurt her?

Ted (*to Ruth*) What are you talking about? I left it in your care

Ruth One of these people has stolen it

Perry We should search the house

  Dora raises the gun at Ted.

Dora You hurt my mum, fuckface

Ted What?

  Ted advances on Dora.

Diana Put it down, right now. It's loaded and it's not a toy

Dora You assaulted my mother

Ted Where's our briefcase?

Dora Stay where you fucking are

Ted Go on then, snotface. Bang – and my ribcage is on the feature fireplace

Dora Don't come near me or I'll fire

Ted No you won't

Ted rips the gun from Dora.

If you want to fire – fire. Fire the bloody gun without a pause

Ted fires, only glancing where his shot will land. He narrowly misses Anton – who is standing in front of the window. The bullet breaks a pane of glass.

Anton Holy fuck – what are you doing?

Diana Are you out of your mind?

Ted These toys are not for little girls

Anton You could've killed me – what the fuck?

Diana STOP IT – ALL OF YOU
What are you doing to my house?

Ripley (*from outside, yelling*) Dora! Dora!

Dora Mum –

Dora runs outside. Isis follows. Anton and Diana look out of the window.

Diana What have you done?

Anton Oh my God

Anton rushes out. Diana follows. Ted and Perry look out.

Perry Fucking hell

Ruth What happened?

Perry He shot the Rev. Oh fucking hell

Perry goes.

Ted I didn't see
Oh Christ

Ruth Are we alone?

Ted I just fired
How was I to know that fucking Rev was there?

Ruth Calm down

Ted Oh Jesus, he's in agony
Oh God, oh God, what have I done?

Ruth Listen to me
Command yourself

Ted He's an old man
He's a fucking priest

Ruth Stop it
This is when you sink or swim
Anyone could see it wasn't your fault

Ted That girl

Ruth It was that girl

Ted Yes

Ruth Be resolute when you are weak
For the man of strong mind is the master

Ted Yes

Ruth Reach for power. He who dares take it is the law-giver

Ted Yes

Ruth And the law makes him right

Ted Ruth

Ruth Manage things
Make them believe
That's your great skill
Make us all believe

Ted is on his knees.

Ted You

Ruth We'll lose everything, unless you get out there
You decide the narrative
And make it into truth

Ted goes. Ruth recovers herself.
The sky darkens. The rain is coming down.
A tapping from upstairs. Ruth stands, silent, galvanised.
A loud creak on the stairs.

Who's there?

Diana and Isis enter, holding the door open. Ted enters
first, as if managing events. Ripley, Anton and Dora
follow, carrying Fiske.

Diana (*to Fiske*) You're doing really well

Ted Put him down by the fire

Diana Everything's going to be fine

Ted Here. Put him here

Ripley Get him in the kitchen. On the table

Fiske Not going to die

Diana Of course not don't be silly you'll be fine

They take him into the kitchen. Isis grabs the first-aid kit
as she passes.

Ted It's just a leg wound, Rev

Anton You're all right

Ted Kids messing with guns

Perry enters the Great Hall.

Perry Look at this blood. Fucking hell, he's bleeding like a
bastard

Ruth Take me to Ted

Perry helps Ruth into the kitchen. Fiske is on the kitchen table.

Ripley Get me light. As much light as you can

Ted Girls shouldn't play with rifles

Isis Shut up

Ripley is putting on surgical gloves. People fetch lights and things to make Fiske comfortable.

Ripley We're going to put you on your side, Dominic. I need to see the exit wound

Fiske Yes, yes

Ted It's probably just a scratch

Ripley Anton. Press your fist down here. Your whole body weight. We have to stop the flow

Anton Do I need gloves?

Ripley No time. Do it now. Right there. Don't move (*To Dora.*) Get the tampons, they're through there. (*To Diana.*) I need your belt to make a tourniquet

Diana Of course

Ted Why did you girls load those guns? Who were you trying to kill?

Ripley (*to Dora*) I might use those tampons to pack the wound. Get them ready

Perry Oh Jesus Ruth, I can't look

Fiske Who fired at me?

Ted (*pointing at Dora*) That young lady. I was disarming her

Dora That's a lie

Ripley Ignore it; he needs calm. (*To Anton, giving him the belt.*) Hold this and pull it, hard

Ted It's an accident, Rev

Ripley Are you a doctor?

Ted No

Ripley Then fuck off

Fiske Feeling awfully cold

Diana (*to Perry*) You, bring that blanket. (*To Fiske.*) We're going to make you warm. I'm sure Ripley's brilliant at these kinds of wounds. She does this every day

Ripley All you need to do is breathe

Dora Mum, I didn't fire it

Ripley I know. I know

> *Diana puts blankets over Fiske. Ripley packs the wound with tampons.*

Isis You're amazing, Dominic. You're going to be fine

Fiske Yes I'm not in that much pain

Isis We'll be playing chess again on Sunday night

> *Ripley speaks only to Diana.*

Diana, the bullet's opened his femoral artery

Diana What does that mean?

Ripley If I can pack and arrest the bleeding, he might stand a chance. I'm not a surgeon

Diana You have my full support

Ruth (*to Ted*) Say something, take command

Ted You'll be up on your feet in no time. You'll get a sermon out of this, I bet

Fiske Ticker
Ticker going all over the place

Isis Your heart's in wonderful shape. It's the loveliest heart I know

Ripley (*to Anton*) Don't move. Keep pulling

Fiske Sweet girl, sweet Isis
    You'll find the sunlight in your life, you will
    You're so lovely
    Some lucky chap will snap you up and make you very
happy

Isis Like you and Michael

Fiske Yes
    Yes

Ripley Hold this. Get me more light

    Perry uses the light on his iPad. Thunder.

Fiske So Ted shot me

Ted No, mate, no

Diana No one meant you any harm

Fiske You must look to your soul, Ted

Ripley Anton, pull harder

    Fiske cries out in pain.

Diana You're doing amazingly well

Fiske Diana, you're a good, good person

Isis You're so brave

Diana You're in expert, expert hands

Perry He's bleeding out

Ted Come on, Rev, you can do it

Ruth We're praying, praying

Diana Think of your favourite place.
  Where would that be?

Fiske Here of course
  With Michael
  Waders on, standing in the river
  Throwing the line
  Birds in the reeds
  The light

Diana Yes, the light here is exceptional

Fiske We cannot have hate

Diana No

Fiske We must resist hate

Isis We will, we will

Ted Come on, woman, fix him

Fiske Ripley, thank you
  We must have love

Ted Breathe

Ripley You're nearly there

Fiske I know
  I'm nearly there
  Michael

  Fiske begins to die. Ruth squeezes Ted's hand,
  determination pouring from her soul. Ripley sees there's
  nothing more that she can do. She gestures to Anton.

Anton CPR – Something – Do his heart

Ripley There's not enough blood left in his body

  Fiske dies. Ripley closes Fiske's eyes. She gives in to her
  distress. Dora comes to her mother's side.

Dora You did everything you could

Diana kisses Fiske on the forehead. She wipes her tears.

Diana My friend
May you rest in peace

Pete enters the Great Hall. He lights a candelabra and takes it to the fire.

Ted I'll walk up the back
And see if there's a signal
Phone the police
Tell them what went down

Isis You're a murderer

Ted We both know that's not true, my girl

Diana Don't do this now

Ted You're grieving and you're just a kid
You're trying to protect your friend
I respect that
But don't be throwing groundless accusations around
Anton, a word

Ted puts his hands on Diana's shoulders and whispers in her ear.

I'm so sorry for your loss

Ted slowly exits into the Great Hall. Ruth suddenly loses all her energy.

Perry Here

Perry escorts Ruth to a chair.

The others, including Anton, lay Fiske out as respectfully as they can.

In the Great Hall, Ted sees Pete surveying the room, an air of Lazarus about him.

Ted You must be Diana's other half
Spent a lot of time trying to find you

Pete Who are you?

Ted Wish I'd found you sooner
Ted Farrier

Pete What're you doing in my house?

Ted Your wife gave us shelter from the storm
Our car's down her lane, sunk in the floods
We saw a light and found our way here

Pete A light shone, did it?

Ted Diana thought you were dead

Pete I'm not dead

Ted No

Pete My heart's beating
I have my faculties.
Dominic Fiske, is he dead?

Ted Yes. Yes, he is

Pete I'm not fond of the man; he's an irritation
But I'm walking up to the house with him and his friend,
this nurse –
And there's a shot – he just crumples like a leaf –
And d'you know what I thought in that second?

Ted No

Pete I thought something had happened to space and time
Like a tear in the fabric
I thought I'd been cloven
Split like an atom
And that I was at the window firing at myself.
I'm not proud but I fled, you understand?

Ted Yeah

Pete Who shot him?

Ted A girl fired the gun

The wind rises.

Pete What girl? Not Isis

Ted No, black kid
I tried to stop her

Pete How?

Ted Someone had to take control. There were loaded guns in here

A door upstairs bangs open. Diana is regarding the corpse.

Diana We have to do what we can for him. I'm going to get him a suit

Diana enters the Great Hall.

Pete Di

In the kitchen, Isis and Anton are helping Ripley and Dora to lay out Fiske. Perry is with Ruth.

Ruth You saw what happened with the gun

Diana Where were you?

Ruth You saw where the blame lies

Perry The girl was aiming it at Ted

Pete I was in the barn

Ruth And she fired

Diana We looked in the barn
We looked everywhere

Perry Yes

Ruth kisses Perry's hand, treasuring him.

I was on the gallery
There were women up there, hiding in the hay

Diana What women?

Pete They've gone now

Diana What hay?

Pete There were horses all around the place last night
  Riding round and round, I could hear them
  Men shouting; a smell of fire

  A door slams upstairs.

That's you, isn't it
  I used to think it was the house
  But you do that

Diana I don't think you're very well

Pete I remember thinking I have to get out
  If I stay in this house, I'll die
  I remember being in the water, rain in my mouth
  Lying there and my insides
  I felt like a chrysalis
  Liquid inside, floating with the flow
  You'd expect it to be freezing but I was hot

Diana You fell downstairs and hit your head

Pete I didn't fall, did I?
  You shoved me
  I was in a fucking shroud

Diana You'd turned on me. You were hurting me

Pete I'd let you go

Diana Something took hold of me and –

Pete You shoved me as hard as you could.
  I got outside and my mind clicked back.
  I knew exactly what you'd done

Ted You're not making any sense, mate

Pete Are you my mate?

Ted I'm a friend of Diana's

Pete Why's he in here?

Diana Because you abandoned me

Ted Do you want me to leave?

Diana No

During the following, Isis enters.

Pete I was always frightened at the tale of Lazarus
The man who came back from the dead
I thought it was horrible
I felt sorry for his wife and kids
Sitting at the table with a man who'd been dead
Whose flesh smelt of earth and fungus and decay

Isis Dad

Pete Are you scared, pet?
I don't blame you

Isis embraces him.

Isis Where have you been?

Perry goes to the door, sees Pete and returns to Ruth.

Pete It's funny how that Bible language stays with you
It's ringing in my ears
I was lost but now I'm found
I lay in the water and it washed me clean

Perry has returned to Ruth.

Perry The husband's back. Pete
He's an all right guy, he's nice to me
Should I tell him his missus was turbo-snogging Ted?

Ruth Was she?

Perry Fucking hell

Perry regrets his words.
    A little more hope abandons Ruth.

Pete I was in the water, drifting in the dark
    Do you want to know what saved me?
    My hand brushed on something soft
    It was a sheep, swimming
    I clung to it
    I turned my body round
    I had to tell my body what to do
    And I realised that the water wasn't deep
    I was in a room
    Wedding barn, of course I know that now
    I was trying to get up to the gallery
    I had this massive feeling there was something I should do
    And then I saw the women there
    They'd been hiding in the stack of hay
    And one of them
    She had an awful, peeling face
    Her neck bent at the nape

Diana This is mad

Pete They were looking at me like I could save them
    Something terrible was coming

Diana Pete, sit down

Pete So many eyes have stared at me like that
    When I was young I'd see them in the crowd
    I'd sing my stirring words
    And inside I'd be empty

Isis Dad

Pete (*to Isis*) I never saved anyone
    I never had a single answer

Isis It's all right

Pete I had to get away from those murdered women
So I walked through a door
I was in a bathroom
A man was there, a spectre
His hair was prophetic and he stared at me
I said 'Are you God or Marx?'
And my own voice came out his mouth
It was a mirror

Ted 'Are you God or Marx?'

Pete I might have passed out then because next thing I
knew I was in the sky and a very tiny child was teaching me
to fly. I looked down. And I could see it all

Isis See what?

Pete Our folly
Our irresponsibility
Our beautiful, spectacular mistakes
Our courage and our ugliness
Our

Isis Our what?

Outside, the storm builds.

Pete I'm sorry, Isis. I'm a very stupid man. Our love

Pete cries. Isis embraces him.

Isis You don't have to have the answers
It's not all on you, Dad
You've always asked the questions and that's good

Diana is moved.

Pete I want to pay my respects to Dominic Fiske

Diana In the kitchen

Pete Don't touch me please

Diana I'm sorry

Pete Is there any love in you?
This house has been my mortuary
And you
You

Pete stops short of accusing her in front of Isis. Isis takes him into the kitchen.

Isis This is Dora

Pete Dora

Ripley This is Anton

Pete Perry, have you been sitting out the storm?

Perry My caravan sunk. That's Ruth

Pete You're all very welcome

Pete pays his respects to Fiske. Diana and Ted are alone.

Ted You know what you must do

Diana I've no idea what I must do

Ted He says you pushed him down the stairs

Diana Something took hold of me. A blind rage, the storm

Ted He's accusing you openly

Diana He's got every right

Ted Attempted murder – why would you let him?

Diana It's true

Diana is consumed with remorse.

Ted There's only a hair between what's false and true.
Truth isn't the argument that's right
It's the argument that wins
Truth is what people can be made to believe

Diana You're Mephistopheles

Ted The original conjuring cat
The greatest magicians have something to learn
From Mr Mistoffelees' conjuring turn

He has brought himself close to Diana.

Sleight of hand
We can both save ourselves

Diana How?

Ted Whatever you say, I will back you up
That man'll never pull you down –
We're going to make each other's truth
Ruth, Anton, Perry, they'll all sing my tune
But the great arbiter of fact is you
The black girl. She shot the Rev

Diana Is that what I must say?

Ted Choose my truth and I'll protect you, I promise

Diana A promise, from a man not bound to truth?

Ted Five million in crowdfunding is yours
I swear I will restore your house
Everything I have is yours

Diana is afraid.

If you want salvation, speak for me

Ted kisses Diana on the neck.

Diana, will you speak for me?

Diana You'll save my house?

Ted The storm may yet take him
I will make you free

Diana I'm going to find a suit for Dominic to wear

She exits upstairs. In the kitchen, Ripley turns to Anton.

Ripley Dominic had faith in you
   He said you broke his heart
   He thought you were worth fighting for

   *Anton turns away and enters the Great Hall. Isis draws
   Pete away.*

Isis That man Ted
   Do you know who he is?

Pete I've a good idea

   *Isis starts whispering to Pete. Ted is wiping his
   fingerprints off the trigger of the gun.*

Anton Sometimes, when a mood descends on you
   It's like you change shape
   Your face and body change
   All day you were festering
   You aimed that gun at me

Ted I don't know what you're on about

Anton It was a warning, wasn't it?
   Next time you won't miss

Ted I didn't fire the gun

Anton We don't need you
   Ruth's the inspiration
   I could lead

Ted (*laughs*) Who'd follow you?
   This is the situation, prick.
   Those little shits have got our case.
   Ruth's the author
   Your name's under mine on every document.
   If they're made public there's no going back
   Our enemies will get us on a terrorism charge

Anton I'm not a terrorist

Ted You signed up to the Tenth Crusade

Anton As a knight

Ted It's not just a fantasy, it's a game plan
It's a campaign of terror and you know it
You don't want to be banged up again
And think about Ruth, languishing inside.
It's the wrong time for your mutiny.
Are you with me, Anton?

Anton I won't stand by and watch you hurting Ruth. You lay a finger –

Ted Back me up and I'll relinquish her

Anton You'll what?

Ted Back me up and I will gift you Ruth

Anton What will Ruth think about that?

Ted She'll do what she's told, won't she
Go upstairs and find the briefcase

Anton My hands are covered in a dead man's blood

Anton goes into the kitchen and washes his hands. Pete has poured shots for the mourners.

Pete Here we are, stormwrecked
What else can we do but raise a toast?

Ripley To Dominic Fiske

They all toast Fiske. Ted enters.

Pete So you're the man who shot him?

Ted It was an accident, like I said. But this girl fired the gun

Isis It wasn't Dora, it was him

Ruth Those girls were pointing guns at us

Perry (*pointing at Dora*) I saw that one fire it. And Ruth did too, except she's blind

Pete So my daughter, who I trust, is telling me one thing and you're telling me another?

Ted She's protecting her friend. I feel for her, I really do

Dora This is bullshit

Ripley Are you honestly trying to blame my child?

Ted Anton, this poor girl. She fired, didn't she

Anton Yes

Dora You're disgusting
You're disgusting

Ripley (*to Anton*) He injured Ruth
He pushed me down
He killed this man
Don't lie for him

Anton turns away. Rain is beginning to hammer down. The wind builds.

Ruth Ted, I'm not well

Dora We've got your briefcase, fucker
We've been reading about your Tenth Crusade
Your war against Islam
Bombs in people's homes and mosques

Isis It's terrorism

Ted That is just ridiculous

Pete Sounds like you're a fascist, Ted

Ted Anton, am I a fascist?
Anton

Anton remains silent. Diana enters. She holds out the briefcase.

Diana This belongs to you, I think. I found it in a wardrobe

Ted takes it.

Ted Thank you so much

Isis Mum, you idiot

Diana I don't want it in my house

Pete How did you let these people in?

Diana Where were you? Pissed up, in a catatonic stupor

Pete Did this man kill Dominic?

Ted The truth, please, Diana

Diana This house is in every breath and cell of me
   I dream about it every night
   I know that you don't understand
   But I smell all my summers in the dust.
   I don't know what that love is called

Isis Just tell the truth

Diana You were born upstairs
   I was alone, crouching in the bathroom
   You, on the floor in ten minutes flat

Isis I know

Diana This house was my midwife

Pete I got back from London
   You were sat there in that chair –
   Sitting right there, with this scrap of humanity wrapped
in a towel

Ted Stay strong and speak the truth
   You and your house will weather this storm

Diana You fired the gun. You fired it

Ted It's strange why you would tell a lie like that

Diana You killed Dominic. The truth

Pete I wish I could have loved this house, the way that I
loved you

Diana You lost faith in me

Pete In myself, in everything –

Diana I was trying to save things

Ted Your lie is understandable – but truth must out
Diana, you could be so much more

Diana I could be sick with shame

Ruth Ted

Ted That adolescent fired the gun
It's delusional to think that it was me

Ruth I want to go

Ted (*yelling*) We can't go
We're staying here
And I will be believed

Ripley Dominic wanted to arrest you
A citizen's arrest for assault
It's manslaughter now.
So Ted Farrier, I arrest you

Ted And do what?

Isis I second you

Ted I don't obey your laws. I write my own

Diana Put him in the yellow room

Ted Are you really going to try and lay a hand on me?
I don't fear jail
I dare to speak the truth
People love my truth
Jail me and I'll become a martyr
My people will be marching outside my cell
Anton, take that to the fire

Anton I'm not your dog. Don't order me around

Ted Perry, burn the contents

Perry Ruth's not well. You should see to Ruth

Pete Don't be fooled by him, Perry; he's a cunt

Perry What help have you ever given me?
They've got answers

Pete They'll fill you full of hate

Ted Burn the papers, mate

Dora We photographed everything, obviously

Isis Your Tenth Crusade, your signatures

Dora (*brandishing her phone*) All your hate crimes, ready
to send

Ted Give me that

Ted comes for Dora. Pete and Ripley stand in Ted's way.

Pete Fuck off

Ted I will have that phone

Ripley Over my dead body

Ruth Ted

Ted Anton, get that fucking phone

*Anton doesn't move. Ted manhandles Pete out of his way.
Ripley stands fast. Diana joins her.*

Ripley Be civilised

Ted Civilisation is far away

*Diana helps Ripley to restrain Ted.
Anton goes to assist the women.
Dora misconstrues and attacks Anton.*

Ruth Ted, take this

Ruth is holding out the knife to give to Ted. Isis joins the fray and disarms her. Perry tries to come forward to protect Ruth.

Pete (*to Perry*) Fucking sit down

Ted Give me that phone
Give me that phone

Anton I'm trying to help your mum

Ted loosens himself. Anton turns his wrath on Ted. They wrestle for mastery.

Ruth There's water coming under my feet; my feet are wet

The deadlock comes apart. The characters realise their predicament; the gravity of the storm. The kitchen is flooding.

Diana The house
We must look to the house

A window bangs open in the gale. The wind roars. The candle flames are flickering out.

We must all protect the house

Slates fall off the roof. Water runs into the kitchen.

They remain, paralysed with fear.

They work to hold back the water, all except Ted. Perry helps Ruth to dry ground. They work together in the deluge, as the gale howls.

Ted stands, ignored, staring at Fiske's corpse.

Blackout.